Letters to the Dead Men

Unexpected Revelations

STACEY GREENE

Copyright ©2018 Stacey Greene
All rights reserved.

Printed in the United States of America

Published by Author Academy Elite
P.O.Box 43, Powell, OH, 43035

www.AuthorAcademyElite.com

All rights reserved. No part of this publication may be reproduced, stored in a retrieval system, or transmitted in any form or by any means—for example, electronic, photocopy, recording—without the prior written permission of the publisher. The only exception is brief quotations in printed reviews.

LCCN: 2018956072
ISBN Paperback: 978-1-64085-424-6
Hardback: 978-1-64085-425-3
Ebook: 978-1-64085-426-0

Table of Contents

Preface vii
1) The Fire Pit 1
2) Summer of '73 7
3) Going Solo 21
4) Montessori to Monticello 37
5) The Five Year Disparity 45
6) There are Mormons at the Door 57
7) Filling the Void 63
8) Best of Show 73
9) Cottage Grove 81
10) Beginnings and Endings 91
11) No More Free Copies 99
12) Powerless 105
13) Regrets 113
14) Noel 119
15) Unexpected Revelations 129

Credits 133
Acknowledgments 134

"Lydia's life serves as a mirror to our own. *Letters to the Dead Men* helps us see ourselves with a new set of eyes."

—Kary Oberbrunner, author of *Your Secret Name, Day Job to Dream Job*, and *The Deeper Path*

Letters to the Dead Men is a story of courage, love, and growing wisdom in the face of losing loved ones. Stacey Greene charts the life of Lydia growing up with her loving family in Cleveland Heights and her course of cognitive loss and their deepening insights into life and death. We were moved and inspired by this heartful and wonderfully honest account of the daily challenges of opening into the unknown. Stacey shares with us the gift of awareness and the grace of love.

—Scott and Ingrid Reichert, chapter leaders
The Compassionate Friends
Geauga and Cuyahoga counties of Ohio

Stacey Greene has put together a collection of remembrances and stories that will take you back to some of the people and events in your own life - that you once knew quite well but forgot as you grew older. Or, at least you thought you'd forgotten... Regard your own journey as you read about Lydia's.

—Dr. Scott F. Wilson, retired pastor.

What a gift Stacey has given us to read. I had the privilege to know personally one of the men that are written about in this work. I now have a renewed level of regard for him and many other people who have passed through my own life, both living and departed. These stories have made me reaffirm my alliances with them and awakened in me an opportunity to feel closer to God.

—F. A. Guy Bauman
LISW – S BCN

Preface

I was privileged to have grown up in Cleveland Heights in the 1970s. It was the first suburb east of Cleveland proper. What a unique place it was; blacks, whites, Asians, gays, hippies and all faiths could live in relative peace compared to other cities in the country at that time.

In addition to being raised with such diversity, I had Ward and June Cleaver parents who were more than anyone could have asked for. They did not drink or swear. I cannot even remember them fighting in front of us four kids. We went to church as a family most Sundays. We came home and ate together or read the *Cleveland Press* newspaper. I can still see Mom at the kitchen table with the coupon section, while Dad was reading some self-help article and my brother Randy and I were fighting over the funnies.

Our parents owned a print shop, so they worked together as well as played together. There was seldom a time when they were apart, and rarely a time when they were not hugging, kissing and laughing. It really set the bar high for me when looking for my own husband later in life.

Perhaps it was because of the love of my parents that I was able to remain somewhat functional when not one, not two, but six of the favorite men in my life died before I turned 40. There were times when I questioned my faith in God, and times when I outright cursed God. There were times when I was stretched to my limits, and times when I really grew in my faith.

This is my story, but with apologies to the reader for some fictionalized pieces. Father Time has robbed me of certain details. Some memories have faded and some were captured from the people who were there during the deaths of these marvelous children of God.

Whether you read this book as a work of fiction or as a woman's memoir is completely up to you. For me, it is a lovely compilation of the variety of individuals who have crossed my path and a continual lesson to love all people, all of the time.

CHAPTER ONE

The Fire Pit

The fire was crackling to perfection. Vince and Nick were true masters. They could get any kind of fire started no matter how damp the wood was from the spring rains.

The Thorpe fire pit was nothing more than some large rocks in a circle behind the pond on the tail end of Lydia and Vince's property; but it was magical to her. What was it about fire pits that brought back wonderful memories? Was it summer camp with s'mores, Grandpa Abe's corn roasting on the outdoor fireplace he built in the old homestead in Pennsylvania, or was it that Lydia and Vince spent years and years of camping vacations always replete with firewood and marshmallows for a romantic evening after a long day of biking and kayaking?

This particular backyard fire pit signified to Lydia a quiet place where she and Vince could enjoy a couple of drinks, listen to some '70s rock playing on the old boom box that they would drag from the garage, and then make out like teenagers. But on this night there would be no make-out session, as what was left of her family had arrived in town for her mother's memorial service. Out came the extra lawn chairs, beer and bags of chips.

One daughter drove up from her college in Arkansas, the other from her college in southern Ohio. Lydia's sister came all the way from California. Lydia and Vince's son, Nick, still lived at home. Nick and his father arranged chairs for themselves and Nick's sisters, Kristen and Kaitlyn. Lydia brought out chairs for herself and her sister, Christy, then returned to the house for marshmallows and a pocket knife for whittling branches to roast the fluffy delights on.

As Kristen tore open the first bag of chips, Lydia returned and grabbed a beer from the ground. Brushing the dirt off of the bottom and wiping the sweat from the can, she popped it open and handed it to Christy. Once settled into their chairs, the conversation naturally went to the subject of Marilyn's memorial service to be held at the end of the week.

Lydia and Christy were relieved at their mother's passing. She had suffered for years from Parkinson's disease and had lost her ability to walk, feed herself or even sit in a wheelchair. She also had every kind of arthritis riddling her frail body and resembled a person with Cerebral Palsy with her hands all curled up and turned inward. Her head was fused to one side and her knees were partially bent no matter how you tried to move her for comfort. The last and most tragic loss of her former self was the ability to speak louder than a groggy whisper, each word pushed out painstakingly with an exhale. So, a typical visit included "Hi, Mom! How are you feeling today?" and her response was "Not... so... good" in a hardly audible murmur. The Thorpe kids knew that Grandma was in a better place while Christy and Lydia found such irony that she passed away on Teddy's birthday.

Teddy was the first of Marilyn's two sons to precede her in death.

"I always thought that when you die Jesus will come and take you home, like in that Relient K song, *Deathbed*. But, maybe Teddy got mom instead and led her to heaven," Lydia remarked.

Christy did not listen to Christian rock and knew nothing of the 11-minute song that can bring an atheist to tears. She cocked her head and said, "Not sure I know that song you are talking about, but yeah, I hope Teddy was there welcoming her to the other side."

With a peaceful look on her face, Lydia commented: "I'm so grateful that I got to do this death right!"

Kristen practically dropped the bag of chips and said "Mom, gross! What do you even mean by that?"

Lydia went on to explain that when Kaitlyn was up for Easter break, they had made a visit to the nursing home. Marilyn was having a really good day. She was even able to squeak out a few words that were perceptible without having to put your ear half an inch from her mouth as she spoke. Lydia was filling her mother in on all of the activities of Christy's children and then began bragging about her own three children. She noticed how alert her mother was that day. Having had much experience with people in her life dying, she remembered that often times those close to death would rally and have a great day very soon before their demise. Lydia took this opportunity to stop boasting about her own kids and tell Marilyn what a wonderful job she had done with all four of her children. Her speech flowed effortlessly as she thanked Marilyn for being a loving mom, a fantastic role model, a great teacher, as well as a playful and giving grandmother to Kristen, Kaitlyn and Nicholas.

Marilyn had looked straight at Lydia with her tiny, bloodshot eyes, crusted over with macular degeneration and cataracts. Lydia remembered how they used to sparkle. They were very light blue like her brother Randy's. He too was gone from this earth but Lydia remembered those eyes that were so blue you could swim in them. Marilyn deliberately looked into Lydia's eyes and asked, "Do you really think I did a good job?"

"Mom," Lydia responded, "you were the best mom anyone could have asked for." She gingerly kissed the few strands of grey (formerly red) hair that still remained on the top of her mother's head.

Something inside one of the burning logs popped and brought Lydia back to the present. The embers from the log sent yellow sparks upward. As Lydia continued to tell the group that she was grateful to have been able to say a heartfelt goodbye to her mom, Vince broke the spell of the story by the hissing of the tab popping on a can of beer. He passed that one to Lydia and reached for his second one.

"I'm glad I said a nice goodbye. I feel like I was robbed of that opportunity with all of my men."

"You mean Teddy, Randy and Daddy?" Christy questioned.

Lydia put her beer down, grabbed two pieces of her brown ponytail and pulled them upward to tighten the rubberband holding her hair off of her face. She said, "Oh Lord, it goes back farther than that. I was obsessed with Grandpa Abe who died when I was 11. Then, right before Teddy died, my friend Charlie from high school died from some weird blood condition. After Teddy's accident, my good friend Aaron died a few years later. Randy and Daddy dying within 5 months of each other was just the icing on the world's most sucky, horrible, death cake. You know, except for Vince and Nick, every significant male in my life has died on me."

Nick looked at his father, speechless.

Christy looked down at the drink in her hand and took a swallow. "Oh, I do remember how close you and Grandpa were. He treated you like his absolute favorite of the four of us. Do you still wear Grandpa's wedding ring? I remember how excited you were that it was offered to you."

Lydia held up her right hand and proclaimed that it had never left her finger since the day her grandmother offered it to her. She twisted the white gold around and around to show her love for it; not because it was gold, but because it was such a cherished memory from long ago.

Lydia scanned the circle of her amazing family as she took another sip. Her daughter, Kaitlyn, always the quiet one of the group, suddenly sat up and asked her mother, "What if you wrote goodbye letters to all of those men?" Kaitlyn loved the letters Lydia had taken the time to write to her while at college. They also texted and called from time to time, but she knew her mother loved to write.

Lydia laughed it off and said, "And addressed them to heaven? Yeah, right! I am sure the postman would think I'm off my rocker."

"No. Don't send them. Maybe somehow on some level, you would just know that you thanked them for being in your life. It could be the closure you need."

"That's actually a cool idea," Christy said. "We do therapeutic writing workshops at my holistic healing center all the time."

"Hmm," Lydia mused.

Lydia noticed Vince and Nick giving each other another look that she could not interpret. Were they smirking or smiling in agreement? As the conversation went back to the memorial service details and fond memories of the children's Grandma, Lydia took another long slurp from the beer Vince had gifted her with. She stared at the blue flashes in the center of the yellow flames of the fire as everyone else began to talk. As Vince placed another log on the fire, the wind changed direction, blasting her face with heat. She moved her chair back and with her left hand, she began twisting Grandpa's ring again. It was a bit large even for her middle finger, so she had developed a nervous habit of playing with it. Around and around she twisted as she thought about just who she *was* and who she had *become*. So many lovely men in her life; each with a specific lesson for her to grasp. Each one showing her a little piece of herself and loving her in a way that only they could. All were taken from her way too soon.

CHAPTER TWO

Summer of '73

Lydia had gotten two of her favorite things for her birthday in the fall of 1972. She received her first Cher album and had practically worn out the song "Half Breed." The appeal of Cher was that she had a show with her husband Sonny, and she sang and told jokes on the show. Lydia's mother often disapproved of the show, as Cher wore such provocative outfits, and Marilyn felt that the humor was a bit off color for her 9-year-old daughter. Still, on occasion they watched it and Lydia's father, Noel, sure seemed to enjoy Cher's crazy outfits.

The second memorable thing Lydia got that year was her first toolkit from her brother Teddy. Teddy was into anything with a motor, and Liddy was into anything that Teddy liked. When he would work on a motorcycle in the garage, Liddy would "work" on her bicycle. She learned from Teddy basic mechanical stuff, and since her father would pick up an occasional junk bike off of a tree lawn on garbage day, she had learned to sand the rust off of the bike frames and repaint them. The toolkit was nothing more than a small, blue metal box with both a Philips head and a slot head screwdriver, a crescent wrench and a few pieces of water sandpaper for removing paint. It wasn't much, really, but it was from Teddy so it was sacred. Randy didn't understand Lydia. He always got her girlie things for birthdays and holidays like dresses or sewing kits, or worse… books!

As the summer of '73 approached, Lydia's sister Christy had the auspicious opportunity to travel to Honduras with the Peace Corps. She had finished college at Western College for Women with straight A's and went to help in Nacaome, Honduras teaching people about nutrition. Christy wondered why she was led into that field as she felt ill-prepared to teach nutrition, but her superiors assured her that if she had ever read the side of a cereal box, she knew as much or more about nutrition than the people she would be working with.

With Christy gone for the summer and Teddy needed at the family print shop, Lydia and her brother Randy would be unattended for most of the summer days while their parents, Marilyn and Noel worked full time. Grandma and Grandpa in Pennsylvania were more than happy to have the two spend the summer with them.

"Lydia? Honey, are you ready? Did you pack your swimsuit?" Mom asked.

"Coming."

"Randy, were you planning on taking all of these books?"

"Yes, Mom. Do they even have a library in Confluence?"

Nerd. Who reads books on summer vacation? Grandma better not have books for me waiting there too. I'll die. I'll just die if I have to do school on vacation.

"Oh, and Liddy? Make sure you bring your writing tablet and workbook. Your teacher said when you get back in the fall she wants to see what you have written about your summer," Marilyn added.

Gosh, I hope she's kidding. What would I write? I swam. I played. I argued with my dumb brother. There. That's my summer.

Summer of '73

The four-hour car ride wasn't too bad. Noel and Liddy loved playing the license plate game where they would try to see how many different state plates they could find. Once they got into farm country and back roads, Dad would always "moo" like a cow and Lydia would pretend that it was a real cow. When she was quite young her father would tease her and tell her that there was a cow underneath the car seat. She could never see Daddy's lips moving when he mooed, so she believed him. Now that she was older, she still enjoyed pretending it was real and laughed appropriately.

Randy only bothered her minimally while they shared the spacious back seat of the station wagon. He busied himself with a book and the occasional wistful look out the window. They stopped once for a potty break and somehow talked their frugal parents into overpriced snacks at the rest stop.

Driving up the hill of Fairview Avenue, Marilyn checked the visor mirror and reapplied some lipstick. The deep red looked so dramatic on her fair skin. She straightened her already perfect rust-colored hair and pushed the snack garbage under the seat. Noel squeezed the behemoth station wagon into the tight driveway and Lydia was the first one out as she went charging into Grandpa Abe's open arms.

"There's my little rascal! Come and give me my hugs. Now, don't forget Grandma too." Grandpa cooed.

Lydia obliged and gave room for Randy to do the same. It did not occur to Lydia to help anyone with any bags or garbage from their snacks. She ran straight away to the back of the house where the chicken coop was. She loved the little bantam chickens and laughed when she heard them cluck and peep. Randy, on the other hand, always proper and genteel, helped with the luggage and opened the front door. He went right into the kitchen and adjoining sunroom to see if there was anything he could help with in the kitchen. He loved to cook, bake and create anything ornate from the most basic ingredients. He was always so imaginative and a wonder to the artistic world. Lydia both resented and respected his talents, for she felt she had none.

After dinner, everyone found a place in the living room and sat around the only TV in the house. It was big and had the bunny ear antenna. The knob to change the channel was broken but you could still turn it if you used the wrench that Grandpa had resting under the set. There were three, possibly four stations to choose from, but Grandma always chose the shows. A Hard Shell Baptist, she usually chose something like the Lawrence Welk Show or The Walton's. Wholesome only. No Sonny and Cher Comedy Hour in that home.

Marilyn and Noel only stayed the night and headed back to Cleveland early the next morning. Lydia sensed that her mother never enjoyed her own mother very much. Years later she found out that it was because her mother was so strict and gave Marilyn a lot of guilt about moving to Cleveland to marry a "city slicker."

Saturday night Lydia tossed and turned still getting used to the sounds of Confluence, Pa. In her suburb of Cleveland, all she ever heard were a few cars and a very rare ambulance in the distance. On Fairview Avenue, she was jolted out of bed several times an evening by the roaring train that was no more than a thousand feet from their home. Sure, the train tracks were fun to walk on and put pennies on to flatten when the trains went by, but the noise of the whistle and clickety-clack of the train cars at all hours were tough to get used to.

Sunday arrived without fanfare. Liddy jumped out of bed at the smell of bacon and tried to ignore the two frilly dresses draped over the chair by her bed. Even though Liddy was allowed to pack her own suitcase this year, she saw that her mother had stuffed a few dresses in for church. *Ugh!*

Liddy's room was right next to her grandparents. It was the designated sewing room with an old-style treadle run Singer and a more modern White brand electric. The rollaway cot was dragged down from the attic for company. The room was directly above the kitchen and she came down the back staircase to see

Grandpa at the stove calling out to her "Now, there's my little sleepyhead. Come and get some breakfast."

Randy came into the kitchen from the dining room, having used the front staircase. He was all polished and eager for church. Grandma said a blessing over the food and the orgy of bacon dripping with fat, fresh bantam eggs and buttered rolls began. The orange juice was fresh squeezed and Liddy and Randy knew by the way the rolls melted in their mouths that they could only have been made by Grandpa Abe. He had a way with those giant hands of his. He knew how to knead that dough and let it rise again and again. His muffins and rolls were better than any store-bought rolls ever could be.

Grandma scolded Lydia for eating too fast and told her she had better get her dress on.

When Grandpa saw her crestfallen face after hearing that she'd have to wear a dress, he excused himself and went upstairs with her, looked at the dresses and pointed to the less frilly of the two.

"That one will do, don't you think darlin'?"

"I guess so," she replied.

Only Grandpa could make her wear a dress without a fight.

Randy handed Grandma a brush and she tore into Liddy's hair as if it had never been combed. When the tears started to well up in her eyes, Randy asked for the brush back and said he could finish for her. It was the first kind thing that Randy had offered to do for Lydia in a while. Or had he always been kind and she did not understand that his gestures were to show affection more than to show off? He took the brush and started working the tangles from the bottom up, slowly and methodically. He seemed to like doing her hair and asked if she wanted a braid or a twist.

Neither. Just leave it alone. Who cares?

"This is the way Teddy taught me how to get tangles out of long hair," Randy said.

"Oh, Randy! She's as pretty as a peach," Grandma cooed.

Marilyn and Noel had chosen to lose the argument over the length of Teddy's hair. He wore it in a ponytail at least seven or eight inches past his shoulders while Randy kept his within the standards of the private school that he attended. Mentioning Teddy made Lydia wonder what he was doing on a sunny Sunday morning. Was he sleeping in, going to the United Methodist church with Marilyn and Noel, or working on a motorcycle? It had only been two days but she missed Teddy already and hoped he would send a letter or call soon.

Hair combed and dress on, Lydia stepped out onto the front porch as Grandpa pulled the 1967 Chevy Chevelle out of the narrow garage. It was Madeira maroon and had plastic seat covers. Lydia tried hard to pull her dress down as much as possible as she climbed into the back seat of the car. Still, when it was hot, the little plastic knobs of the seat protectors would leave impressions on the backs of her legs and she felt like her skin was ripping off if she jumped out of the car too fast.

The drive down the street, over the train tracks, across the bridge and around the corner to the Turkey Foot Valley Baptist Church on Sterner Street took no more than six or seven minutes, but it was enough time for Grandma to remind Lydia to mind her manners and sit still. They arrived early, as Grandma played the organ and needed to get there early with her music. Grandpa let her off at the door and she started up the concrete stairs. A stiff wind took her sheet music and several sheets seemed to have sprouted wings. Randy was the first to jump out and help collect the music and hand it back to Grandma as she bounded up the remaining stairs. Lydia thought Grandma was quite spry for a woman in her early 70s. Lydia stayed with Grandpa as he parked the car. He took her little hand and walked into the sanctuary of the church.

The pews were long and wooden. The seat cushions were made from the scratchiest red fabric imaginable. Lydia assumed it was to keep everyone awake during the long service. To a 9-year-old girl, sitting in church for more than an hour on a sunny day just didn't seem fair. The stained glass windows were cracked open for a breeze and there were two oscillating fans, one on each side of the back of the church. Grandpa knew to sit between Randy and Lydia to stave off any poking and pinching during the service. Randy, being six years her senior, usually sat still and went right to work on the children's insert of the program unless he wanted to bug his sister for fidgeting. He solved the riddles and colored in the cute drawings, often adding his own adornments to the drawings of the apostles and their robes.

Grandma played the first hymn, "The Old Rugged Cross." Lydia tried to understand the lyrics but it sounded really depressing with words like "shame," and how sinners were slain, and something about laying down trophies. Her mind wandered to winning a trophy someday but she had no idea what talents she would ever be good enough to win one with. Randy seemed to be paying rapt attention as the sermon began. Lydia stared at her grandfather and slipped her little hand inside of his. She marveled at how big his hands were and how funny it was that old men had hair on the backs of their hands. She ran her index finger across his thumb fingernail. Why was it so rippled like a piece of corrugated cardboard, she wondered. The edges of most of his fingers had cracks all around the nails and the occasional hangnail. She knew he was a farmer and assumed that it must be hard work. As her hand slid underneath his, she felt callouses on the underside of his hand. She looked at his wedding ring. It looked silver. It was thin. Her father's was thick and gold but she liked this one. Grandma had bragged about how it was not silver but a white gold. That seemed like an oxymoron to her. How could gold be white? It didn't even look white, but silver to her. Grownups were weird.

The service continued but Lydia could not get interested in any part of it as long as her legs kept itching from the fabric of the pews and her dress kept riding up. She swung her legs back and forth, back and forth under the pew and stared at the sun coming through the stained glass windows. At the end of what seemed like forever and a day, the final hymn played. Grandpa broke out in a joyous voice as he whispered to her "This one is my favorite."

"How Great Thou Art" instantly became her favorite too as she listened to his crackly, old voice sing about nature. She loved how the song sang about being grateful for the stars, the rolling thunder, the whole universe. She marveled at how this hymn was so much fun, singing about woods and mountains and breezes and brooks. Abe seemed to get a drop or two of water in his eyes when he sang about the sacrifice Jesus made and she wondered about the word "scarce" as he sang "I scarce can take it in…" At the end of the hymn, there was a benediction from the pastor and Grandma played one more song as the people left the sanctuary.

Their grandmother was so proud to show the kids off to all of her old cronies, but Lydia just wanted to be out in the sunshine. She found it hard to make eye contact with adults and thought it totally unnecessary to tell everyone her age and grade. Did they really care? Grandpa, quick to sense her hyperactivity, asked Grandma if he could take Lydia out to get the car with him. Randy loved the attention of the older ladies and he stayed to talk as well as hold Grandma's arm going down the steep steps of the church. The short ride home was interrupted by an unusually long train passing before they could turn off of the bridge and onto their avenue.

Randy helped in the kitchen while Lydia sat in one of the two, tall, matching rocking chairs in the sunroom. Her legs pushed back and forth, back and forth, back and forth anxiously awaiting lunch. Grandma was quick to scold her for not helping and Randy was quick to announce that she never did because of what a spoiled baby she was. Tears began welling up in her eyes but she dared not cry. This would only prove his point and allow him to call her more names. Randy never called her a "dummy" or an "idiot." Oh no, his vocabulary was off the charts for a young teen. He preferred to ridicule with insults like "impudent shrew" or "skunk breathed Leviathan." Liddy had no idea what a Leviathan was and had never seen a shrew, but Randy's tone of voice said all she needed to know.

Most of Sunday was spent eating, clearing the dishes, wiping down the table and enjoying the backyard of the property, just shy of the fence where the chickens ran. Sunday was God's day and neither Grandma or Grandpa worked much other than meal preparation. Grandpa helped Grandma put the leftovers away. He pulled old tin foil out of a junk drawer and with loving hands smoothed out a piece that must have been used at least a dozen times. He gently put it on top of the container and placed it in the refrigerator. In that junk drawer were all sorts of treasures. There was a ball of twine, a ball of rubber bands, matchbooks, candle stumps, bread ties, a flashlight, a pocket knife, toothpicks, pencil stubs and a few other oddities.

Randy read a book for a while until a spider crawled across his leg. He let out a shriek and jumped from his chair. Abe walked over and picked up the tiny creature and took it outside.

"Why didn't you step on it, Grandpa?" Liddy wanted to know.

"Well, I reckon he's one of God's creatures just like us."

"I got bitten by a spider in my sleep one time. My eye swelled shut. I would have stepped on him," she said proudly.

"Well, I would never step on you my little rascal."

The house on Fairview Avenue was a simple home with an extra room on the first floor that held both a piano and an organ for Grandma to practice on. It made them sound so fancy to have a music room. Randy retired to the music room to practice the piano. When Grandma asked if Liddy needed to practice, she groaned. How could Lydia ever get to the exciting pieces that Randy could play? Randy bragged about how much fun the Bach two part and three part inventions were to play. "They are called 'sinfonias'," he told Grandma. Even if she already knew that she acted impressed. Lydia took a turn later, but only played two pages from the *My Piano Adventures Level 1* book and became incredibly bored slamming her little fingers on the keys. Seeing weird black notes on a lined page was too much like reading.

The following days were spent much the same. Randy, ghostly white, overweight and not athletic, preferred to stay indoors and help Grandma in the kitchen. Lydia spent most of her waking hours in the sunshine. She loved to help Grandpa scatter the feed across the chicken run, and although she was scared when they came too close to her, she liked the little hens.

Helping in the garden was pure bliss. Grandpa never scolded her if she put the seeds too close together. He just explained one more time as if it was his very first time telling her. Corn was her favorite. The seeds were big and easy to drop into the little rows Grandpa had made. He always set a goal of "knee high by the fourth of July" for the best roasting ears.

Carrots, lettuce and kale had tiny little seeds that had to be neatly scattered in the rows and later thinned out when they popped out of the earth. Grandpa already had plenty planted before the children's arrival, but he let Lydia plant a small area with the extras, just for her to see the variety of God's wonder. Onions were fun to plant because they came in what were called "sets" so as Liddy plopped them in, she could pack the dirt around with just a little green shoot sticking out and see exactly how many she had planted that day. Grandpa explained that these onions were planted too late and would only be small at best by the end of the summer. Still, he must have left some for June planting simply for Lydia.

By the time she and Randy had arrived in Pennsylvania, the spinach and lettuces were already able to be picked for salads. Grandpa started them earlier in the season in boxes that he made out of old windows with hinges on one side to open up and pick. She thought her Grandpa was a genius to make these mini greenhouses from old windows. The tomatoes were planted next to basil to keep the insects away and make the tomatoes sweeter. There were chives everywhere. Many consider them to be weeds, but Grandma used them in almost all of her dishes. Lydia had a funny trick of eating them raw and coming up to Abe to give him a stinky breath kiss. He never minded her sense of humor and knew her to be way too sensitive to do the same back to her.

Summer squash had to have full sun and lots of room. Peas had long poles to grow up on. Lydia helped hold the jute string as Grandpa Abe stretched it up and down the poles at either end of the pea row. Bush beans had smaller sticks as markers and Liddy begged for pumpkins, even though Grandpa said the pumpkins would not be ready by the time the kids went back to Cleveland. Dill was also all around the property and no potato salad was complete without fresh dill.

Grandma enjoyed pretty flowers in the part of the garden where she could see them from her sunroom. Grandpa interspersed herbs and flowers in this area so that Grandma could enjoy both the flowers and snip off fresh herbs for cooking. He and Lydia tended to the random and somewhat chaotic mish-mosh of red and yellow columbine, bay, black cohosh, thyme, mint, violet dwarf-crested iris, Virginia bluebells, Culver's root, yarrow and oregano. Liddy was dizzy trying to remember all of the names of the plants and when they were to bloom. From living in Cleveland, she already knew that crocuses only came in the early spring, giving way to daffodils and tulips. By fall they would be long gone but then her mother would place chrysanthemums all over their property on Hampshire Road.

The front of Abe and Nina's property had snapdragons, black-eyed Susan's, Hydrangeas, and in pots were petunias of all colors, dripping down the planters. The front porch had two outdoor folding chairs and a chaise lounge that always caught the fabric of unsuspecting people as they got up from lounging. The wood floor had a slat that was warped and the side of the porch closest to the garage had overgrown tree branches that were encroaching onto the porch.

One morning Grandpa asked Liddy if she wanted to go and "fetch" some water with him. She never understood why he walked more than a mile through the woods, mostly uphill to get water when it came right out of the tap in their home. Still, she enjoyed a good nature walk and a chance to leave the breakfast dishes for Randy to help Grandma wash and dry. The two began their trek past the chicken run and into the woods. Grandpa called that hill Gum Boot Hill. The pricker bushes nipped at Liddy's ankles and Grandpa showed her poison ivy at a distance.

"Leaves of three, let them be," he told her.

"Why are we getting the water from the spring, Grandpa?"

"Oh, darlin' wait til you taste the difference."

And that was all they said for the next 15 minutes. Grandpa stopped her once and put his index finger up to his mouth to indicate a "shhh." He pointed and there at the stream was a deer and her little doe. The mother's ears were twitching back and forth as her head darted here and there, watching for danger as she and her spotted baby had a lovely drink. The water moving along the rocks was magnificent. The sounds of the babbling brook made Lydia think of the hymn Grandpa Abe had belted out at church. They smiled at each other as they watched the deer run away. They lowered their gallon containers down into the running spring until they were full. The walk back, although mostly downhill, was difficult for Lydia with little fingers lugging heavy glass, gallon jugs of water.

Summer marched on, getting hotter and hotter with each day. Craving a trip to the Youghiogheny Dam, Liddy began the pleading, begging and whining to go and swim. Nina was afraid of water and Randy would wilt in the sun. Her frequent begging won out and the rectangular styrofoam floatie came out of the cellar. It had a net in the middle so that unsuspecting swimmers would not fall through while lounging in the water. It fit nicely between the siblings in the back seat of Chevrolet, which Grandma pronounced "Chiv–A–Lay."

Grandma never let Liddy go as far out as she wanted to, but it was water and sun, so she didn't complain. Besides, even Grandma loved a soft-serve ice cream at the Tasty Freeze at the bottom of the hill of the dam when swimming time was finished. Randy always had to put extra sunscreen on his multiple scars on his lower legs. Four surgeries were performed on him during his elementary school years to fix his bilateral clubbed feet. The doctors took tendons in his lower leg and switched them to pull straight and not inward. Liddy was too young to remember the braces and casts, but she did remember the couple of years that Randy wore orthopedic shoes to make sure the surgeries stuck. Now, his scars would always burn if he wasn't vigilant with the sunscreen, which at the time only had an SPF of about 8.

One afternoon Grandpa took Lydia to the feed store for chicken feed. The drive up and down the mountains was always a bit frightening for her. There were so many times where you could not see the road ahead until you were right up on top of the crest. On occasion, Grandpa knew the smaller hills well enough to charge up the peak and then let off the gas as the car went down. Her tummy would flip and flop as if on a roller coaster. She giggled and asked him to do it again.

The highlight of the summer was when her grandparents took the two children to the Somerset County Fair in Meyersdale.

"Now Randy, you and Lydia stick together. We are not going to chase you around all day. Grandpa and I are going to see a few of the exhibits. Meet us back at the picnic tables by 2. You hear me, young man?"

"Yes, Grandma."

"Now, here is the money for the rides and some snacks. You may each get six tickets. When you get back here we will have lunch, so don't fill up on sweets."

"Ok," he lied.

Grandma never let the children have pop or sugary cereals during their summers there, but with their new found wealth they rode a few rides and indulged in cotton candy, elephant ears and large, sugary lemonades with the full pieces of lemons in them. Liddy enjoyed a few rides with Randy, but neither of them enjoyed being at the top of the Ferris wheel when the people on the bottom were getting on or off.

When the money had run dry, they went to see where their grandparents were. Grandpa was in the barn with the goats while Grandma was talking to some ladies in the shade outside of the barn.

"Did you have fun, precious?" she asked Liddy.

"Yes, but my tummy hurts."

"Shhh!" Randy said. He wasn't sure Grandma would approve of the food choices.

"Come on Abe, we'd better get that lunch before the potato salad turns," Grandma said.

Toward the second week of August, the children of Confluence returned to school. Not that Randy and Lydia had many friends their own age on a street that only had 12 or 13 houses on it. Still, it felt lonely when they saw the school bus meander up the hill each morning and two or three children with book bags hopped on. They were about ready to return home, even though Cleveland schools did not start until the Wednesday after Labor Day.

Randy had run out of books and Liddy was sick of the workbooks Grandma had made her complete. Nina was a retired school teacher. Thirty-four years of teaching kindergarten through grade two must have been a hard habit to let go of, for she loved coercing Liddy into page after page of material meant for the school year. If Lydia ever saw another red correction pencil, it would be too soon.

CHAPTER THREE

Going Solo

Lydia was not looking forward to leaving the next summer. Her parents had told her that she was "flying solo." Randy was old enough to help at the print shop and she would be all alone with her grandparents. As much as she did not get along with her brother, he did on occasion play with her. Usually, though, he just made her feel inferior. Like the time there was a pirate ship on the back of the cereal box. When the box was empty, the instruction said to cut here and fold there then insert tab A into slot B. Liddy wished with all of her heart that she could make that pirate ship, but alas, Randy had much better manipulative skills and did not trust her with scissors. As the artist he was, it came out flawless and wonderful. It was a simple, cardboard pirate ship but it looked so realistic and was now his since he had made it.

I like Grandma and love Grandpa, but who will go on the rides with me at the fair? Oh Gosh! I bet Grandma has books for me to read and workbooks for me to complete. Not again.

Liddy knew Grandma had scores of academic bridge activities for her. The sad thing was, often they were not even bridge activities but more like remedial activities to catch her up with her brilliant siblings. Some said she may have fallen behind because she had skipped kindergarten so that her parents could work full time starting their print shop. They needed her occupied all day so they enrolled her in a Montessori school run out of a nearby synagogue. This particular Montessori was a new school in the area and gladly took her at the age of 5 for first grade. Her grandmother thought she was behind because of "that newfangled Montesorri nonsense." Liddy just figured that she wasn't smart and really didn't care about anything that involved sitting still.

Her sister, Christy, landed in the top tenth of one percent on the National Merit Test. She was an actual winner and attended college for free. Next came Teddy, her favorite brother. Teddy looked tough, cool and rode a motorcycle, but was deep, insightful and a great writer. Now 19, he could usually be found under the hood of a car or some other machine, making it run like new. He also fixed printing presses, cameras and anything with moving parts. Randy had the most amazing vocabulary and tied with Christy for being the most verbose. His artistic talent surpassed all of the other family members put together. It did not matter the medium. Painting, perspective drawing, sculpting, sewing, baking or even theater arts… all came naturally to him. His creativity had no limits and life to him was just something to embellish and decorate.

Lydia was told by Grandma that her mother, Marilyn, was second in her class in high school and won a scholarship to Mather College (now part of Case Western Reserve University). Her father was an English teacher at a private college preparatory school for years before becoming a printer. He bragged that his classes always had the highest SAT English scores in the entire school.

So where did Lydia's talents lie? Were there awards for who could stay outside the longest and bring home the nastiest sunburn blisters? Did anyone hold a well-paying job of starting but not finishing books? Could she make a living being a whining, tattletale? Still, in the deep recesses of her mind, she knew that the joy of being a kid was all about running, jumping, screaming, laughing, swimming, biking, tree climbing and playing. She knew she was not the deep intellect that her family members seemed to be, so she busied herself with the things she was good at.

There were several steps leading up to the porch of the mini Tudor home they lived in on Hampshire Road. The steps, porch floor and surrounding walls were all cement or stone. Lydia loved jumping from the top of the wall onto the driveway of her neighbors. The more her mother, Marilyn, would look horrified at the height, the more Lydia would get a thrill out of jumping off of it. That was her talent.

Money ebbed and flowed in their home, as most small business owners can attest to. When times were lean and her father told her "no" to a new skateboard; Lydia just asked Teddy for some tools and an old piece of wood. She took apart some old-style, metal roller skates that formerly went over shoes and made a crude skateboard that actually worked. She figured that if her Grandpa could make soap out of pig fat, or a greenhouse out of old windows, she could make a skateboard out of skates. That was another talent.

Riding bicycles was her favorite activity. Her father was always on the lookout for a tree lawn special on garbage day. Liddy had a hand-me-down blue bike given to her by her older and more well-off cousins. This year, things must have been prosperous at the print shop because while packing for the summer's trip to Confluence, they packed her new, store-bought, pink bike with the high rise handlebars like the real Schwinn Stingrays. She did not care that it most likely came from Kmart; it had streamers hanging from the handgrips. Teddy had shown her how to tape a playing card to the front fork to spin across the spokes and sound like a motorcycle while she rode.

Lydia idolized Teddy with his long, hippie hair, red-tag Levis jeans and fingernails filled with dirt from fixing cars and motorcycles. He had a smile that could melt butter and always had just the right amount of British Sterling Cologne on. She made a point to sniff his neck when he hugged her and she knew she would miss him the most that summer as they made the 4-hour drive with her parents from Cleveland Heights to Confluence to drop her off.

Lydia also wanted to stay in Cleveland Heights to run with her father. Earlier in the year, Noel had a scare at his doctor's appointment. He was told to start running or die. Yes, he was overweight, but she liked his belly and used to call it her pillow. In the evening when the family would gather around the television to watch the prime-time shows, Lydia would lay by her father and rest her head on his belly and enjoy the show or drift off to sleep with the rise and fall of his protuberance.

When Noel began to run (or jog), he could barely make three houses up the street. Eventually, he made it around the block, which was about a half a mile. Initially, he hated running. He asked his overly active daughter, Lydia, if she would like to come with him to keep him company. She took to running like a duck to water. She was built more like a sprinter, with large hamstring muscles, short legs, longer torso and thick calves; but she loved the conversations she and her dad would have on these morning runs. Her father began to enjoy running as the pounds started melting off of him, fifty in all. By the summer between middle school and high school, Lydia would become bored with the weekend 10K race and run in full, 26.2-mile marathons. But for now, another summer in Pennsylvania, going solo, loomed overhead.

Randy and Teddy made the drive out to Pennsylvania with Lydia for a short visit to see Nina and Abe. The grandparents were waiting on their porch when the family, sans Christy, rolled up the narrow driveway of Fairview Avenue. After the perfunctory hugs and kisses, Nina was barking out commands to Abe and micromanaging the visit as usual. Lydia's first order of business was to go to the dining room and see if Grandma had filled the glass candy dish. She helped herself to one and stuffed her pockets with a few more before anyone could see. She stared up at a poem that had always been there, but this was the first time she actually read it. Framed in a faded green with the paper yellowed with age she read the handwritten poem.

> "My father could not make a poem,
> But setting his course by yonder pine,
> Straight and true he plowed a line
> Across the field.
> My father could not juggle words,
> But with the birth
> Of golden wheat in summer sun,
> He coaxed a poem out of the earth."
> By Mary Ferrell Dickinson

She was startled when she felt her father's hand on her shoulder. He grabbed a cellophane wrapped candy and said, "Isn't that a great description of Grandpa? It always reminds me of him."

The following morning Lydia tried hard not to cry as she saw Randy and Teddy get into the car. Her father hugged her tight and whispered, "Don't worry my dear, sweet, little, white rose... you'll have fun. But I'll really miss my running partner!"

Summer was long and hot that year. Abe was no longer raising his chickens and gardening had lost some of its appeal because he only planted what the family would use. Liddy spent most of her time on her pink bike until one day when she miscalculated the sharp right turn at the bottom of the street. The large hydrangea bushes at the bottom of the hill had recently been pruned and as Liddy slid into the bluish haze of flowers she let out a howl. Assessing the damage to herself, she saw a branch in her leg. Leaving her bike there, she pulled the stick out and ran with breakneck speed back up the street and into Grandpa's arms. The blood was racing down the hole in her leg as Grandpa stoked her hair and kept repeating, "There, there, now darlin'. there, there."

An expert at a calm demeanor, Grandpa patched her up, dried her eyes with his worn, red handkerchief and helped her climb gingerly onto his lap. He rocked her in the sunroom and stroked her head some more as he sang "Hinkey Dinkey Parlez Vous," but he always changed the words to "Hinkey Dinky Doo Dum Day."

Just as the summer before, Liddy spent some time begging her grandparents to take her to the Youghiogheny Dam to swim. Grandma was still paranoid about Lydia drowning, so she always had to stay near her styrofoam floatie with the net now stretched out from overuse.

Her grandfather was the only one she ever knew born prior to 1900. He had helped build that dam during the Roosevelt Administration. Liddy wondered if he was reminiscing those days as he stared out at the thousands of rocks that made up the dam. He had also told her a story she wasn't entirely sure that she should believe. He said that before the lake that she was swimming in actually became a lake, there used to be a town called Somerfield there.

"They must have had 'bout 150 people who all had to move after the flood of 1936. Sometimes when the water level is really low, you can see a part of the bridge."

"What bridge?" she wondered.

"It was the National Road, Route 40 and I 'spect it's about 60 or 70 feet down. Oh, the town had Hooks Restaurant, and a tire store, grocery store and the like. If I recollect, the original bridge was built around 1818."

Even though Grandpa's story said that they all had to leave after the flood so all of the dams could be built, it creeped her out a little thinking she could be swimming on top of a real town.

"Let me look at that leg little darlin'," he said, staring down at the hole where the tree branch had attacked her. "Yep, I thought so. You won't leave well enough alone and stay out of the water long enough for a scab to heal. Back in the barn, I've got something."

Sure enough, the giant scab from the earlier bike crash kept forming then floating away in the dam. Once home, Abe dug out some Porters Linament Salve from the barn. It was used for horses as well as people and came in a greenish, round tin rusted and weathered with age. Liddy hated the smell. It was thick like peanut butter but seemed to finally waterproof the hole in her leg long enough to allow a scab to form. To this day, the scar on her thigh is a reminder of that sunny summer with her favorite grandparent.

On occasion, Grandpa sent Lydia down to the cellar. She called it a basement but in the country, it was a cellar. It always seemed so sinister as she went down the creaking, wooden stairs. Whether it was canned peaches or elderberry jam he sent her down for, she was always quick to come back up. Grandma always had canned goods she and her friends "put up" each year. They sat on shelves that were nothing more than long slats of warped wood. She took a second trip downstairs to get the big blocks that Abe had made from an old tree. She knew she was a bit old too old for blocks, but she loved building tall towers just to knock them down. She also made houses for her Barbies and used spools from Grandma's sewing kit and cardboard from old cereal boxes to create furniture. She knew she was getting too old for Barbie doll play, but who was judging? Lydia used to complain about not getting real Barbie doll furniture, but honestly, it made her more creative and she did take some sense of pride in her creations.

In addition to the school time Grandma insisted on, she also taught Lydia the basics of crewel embroidery. The pride from learning how to execute a perfect French knot and have Grandma complement her on her satin stitch made all of that sitting still worth the effort. Her first sampler was a series of purple and blue flowers with intense green stems. Nina also let her use any of the fabric scraps that were in her scrap bag, so Lydia began making crude attempts at Barbie doll clothing too.

Nina and Abe went out of their way to try to find a girl Lydia's age to play with that summer, so there were occasional playdates with a girl with striking red, curly hair. Lydia did not think she had anything in common with her, but tried to make the best of it and worked hard to understand her thick, southern drawl. They rode bikes, played with Barbie dolls and listened to vinyl 45's on the record player that Grandma had used years before in her classroom. The records were as old as the hills. The 1970s were a time of women in the workforce, the Mary Tyler Moore Show, and females really starting to step into male-dominated jobs. Yet, here Lydia and her new friend Leslie were listening to songs like "Buckwheat Cakes" by Buddy Ebsen and Darlene Gillespie. It was quite popular in 1958 and was all about a woman winning her man over with her chocolate cake, Irish stew, and buckwheat cakes along with crispy bacon. The girls also sat by the record player and listened to the soundtracks of "Bedknobs and Broomsticks" and "Jungle Book." Lydia was too shy to dance in front of her friend, but when she listened to the "I Wanna Be Like You" track in private, she always went wild, pretending to be the big ape.

Lydia taught her new friend Leslie how to play Jewish Jacks or Kugelach. It was harder than regular jacks as there was no ball. The playing pieces were little blocks. Leslie taught Lydia variations on regular jacks. They played Chinese Checkers and walked along the railroad tracks by the bridge at the end of the street.

Lydia had no need for an alarm clock. Her alarm clock was her grandfather's voice. No doubt he had already been up for hours. "Lydia, darlin', are you awake?" Grandpa called one morning.

"Yes, sort of."

"Well, now, Grandma has some chores for you to do and she says you forgot to finish your math worksheet last night."

"Coming," she said as she threw on the same clothes she had on the day before.

"Lord-have-mercy!" Grandma cried. "You keep wearing the same clothes and they are going to walk right off of you!" she continued.

"Let's let her eat first," Grandpa said, as he pulled out the chair for her.

Liddy reached for the juice and felt a light smack on the top of her hand.

"Hold your horses," Grandma barked. "We didn't pray."

Grandpa mumbled a quick prayer and looked as excited as Lydia to tuck into a hearty breakfast. Liddy ate and ate and Grandma noticed.

"Why you'll be as full as a tick if you're not careful."

When the breakfast dishes were in the sink, Liddy started tearing up old undershirts for the rag pile. They also took the old tea towels and turned them into rags. Next, she and Grandpa hung the recently washed clothing out to dry on the line in the backyard. Grandma owned a dryer, but Lydia had rarely seen her use it.

Back inside, she found her Grandma taking out the coffee filter from the coffee maker and rinsing it gingerly. She placed it over a cereal bowl turned upside down in order to dry it for reuse. She also reused tea bags until the third cup of tea had no taste and looked like nothing more than dirty water.

Nothing was ever wasted. Tin foil, twine, rubber bands, the twist ties that came on bread, plastic food containers all had a purpose beyond its original intention. Lydia wondered why they spent so much effort doing all of these things. Back at home, her own mother was always at the print shop and they often opted for convenience over the toil of her grandparents. One time her mother had tried to explain to her about how they lived through the Great Depression, but when it sounded like a history lesson, her ears just rolled right up.

The quilts were the only thing Liddy really enjoyed the history of. You see, Grandma Nina and her quilting cronies would cut up old house dresses and make the most beautiful quilts. It was fun recognizing the dresses Grandma wore. Each one had a particular pattern. She loved the double pinwheel and the bear's paw the best; but Grandma had it in her head to make the Sunbonnet

Sue pattern for Lydia that year. Lydia was not actually allowed to use it yet.

"Why did you make it if I can't use it?" Lydia queried.

"Oh, my eyes are going and I don't know if I will even make another one. You save this and take good care of it to remember me by."

That sounded incredibly morbid, and Liddy didn't like the pattern or the bright yellows in it, so she ran off to play outside and never gave it another thought until years later when she realized that it was indeed the last quilt Grandma ever made.

Lydia spent other days with Grandpa Abe, sitting next to each other in matching rocking chairs one of Grandpa's relatives had made. Liddy was nonstop back and forth, back and forth while she asked her Grandpa dozens of questions and chattered away like a mynah bird. Poor Abe must have learned how to just zone out and say "Ah, yes. Interesting." The two of them played a game until her energy was more than a man in his late 70s could take.

"Darlin' how many times can you count to ten and back without taking a breath?" he would ask. And off she went, taking a large breath and going "One, two, three, four, five, six, seven eight, nine, ten, nine, eight, seven, six, five, four, three, two, one, two, three…" until her face turned red and she finally wore herself out.

Toward the end of summer, all of the family, even Christy, arrived in Confluence for the annual family reunion, about a half-hour away. When time came to divvy up who went in what car, Randy, always the goody-two-shoes rode with the grandparents while Lydia rode with her parents, Christy and Teddy, whom she had missed dearly that summer. It was held at a church pavilion on the top of a hill near Ohiopyle.

As they pulled into the narrow, pea gravel driveway, many women were already arranging the food on the various picnic tables, all lined in a row. The pavilion was large enough for two long rows of tables. One row of tables was for the food and the other was for the guests. A group of pot-bellied men, most of whom were wearing overalls or jeans with suspenders, was gathered at the far end of one of the tables laughing and slapping thighs about something or other. She recognized a couple of great uncles, but honestly, she could never keep straight the plethora of great aunts and uncles.

Grandma Nina had come from a family where her father had married a woman named Jenny. She had seven children then passed away. Nina's father later remarried another woman, coincidentally also named Jenny, and had six more children. This was the batch of children where Grandma Nina came into the picture. On Grandpa Abe's side of the family, there were 14 children, but only seven lived past infancy. To further complicate the genealogy for Lydia to remember, the farms were so close where the families grew up that more than one sibling from the one family married a sibling from the other family. Farm life at its finest in southern Pennsylvania.

Many of the relatives were from farther south, amplifying the southern drawl of so many. They came from Virginia, Maryland, West Virginia and Tennessee. Lydia's family and a few others were from Ohio and one distant cousin came from Michigan. There was always too much food. Southern comfort foods were abundant as Lydia walked down the long picnic tables deciding which macaroni and cheese looked the most appetizing. Potato salad, several kinds of fried chicken, deviled eggs, brownies, cookies, homemade pies and BBQ ribs were only a fraction of the cornucopia available to the 80 plus people in attendance. The only healthy thing on her plate was the cucumber and onion salad she helped Grandma make with sour cream, vinegar, salt and sugar.

There were children Lydia had no interest in getting to know and games scheduled for them after the feeding frenzy.

I'm not playing the dorky games this year. I'm not a baby. If Teddy isn't playing them then I'm not. It's just a bunch of hicks. Most of them talk hillbilly and I can barely understand what they are saying!

But in the end, their mother, Marilyn, coerced Lydia and Randy to play a few of the games so they did not appear to be the snobs from the north. They played balloon toss, a three-legged sack race and one game where players had to carry an egg on a spoon in relay fashion without breaking the egg. Truth be told, the competitive side of Liddy was awakened and she ended up having fun.

When the bellies were all stuffed and the games played, the grownups had their annual meeting about boring things like who died that year, where the next year's reunion would be and so on. All Lydia wanted to do was go for a walk with Teddy. Leaving Christy and Randy behind, they hiked around for a bit and just talked. He had missed her as much as she missed him. He was so animated about the latest car he was working on and how he was dating a new girl, Sue. He tousled her hair and said, "Hey, I made this for you."

"Cool!"

"Yeah, Sue taught me how to braid these bracelets from cord. Here, check out mine," he said as he showed that his was just the same.

"Let's get back before Grandma starts barking at us," he reminded her.

They made their way out of the wooded area and back into the sun as the grownups were finishing up.

When all of the paper plates were thrown out, Tupperware lids put on empty containers and goodbyes said, they made the drive up and down the hills back to Confluence. Liddy was so eager to get back to Cleveland Heights and to have Teddy sitting next to her on the ride home, that she barely even remembered saying goodbye to her grandparents.

In February of 1975, Abe Skinner died from a stroke. It was a cold and snowy day, and 911 was not available in Somerset

County until the early '90s. The central dispatch did its best, but navigating hills and railroad tracks to get to the nearest hospital did not help Abe's chances of survival. Liddy was in Cleveland Heights at the time, attending her Montessori school, beating all of the girls and some of the boys in gym class and learning Hebrew. She was working hard at not falling too far behind academically, but the only books she enjoyed reading were the *Little House on The Praire* series by Laura Ingalls Wilder. She knew that if her mother did not think she had advanced to where she should be, then the next summer Grandma would give her another slew of drill and kill exercises crammed with seemingly useless facts like state capitals and multiplication tables.

The news of her grandfather's passing was hard on Lydia, now 11. It was the first death she had experienced and she secretly lamented that her favorite of the four grandparents went first. The drive back to Pennsylvania for the funeral was somber as the snow fell and the roads were icy. Grey clouds hung over most of the drive out of Ohio and four hours felt like 20.

The service was at the Humbert Funeral home in Confluence with the internment at Indian Creek Baptist Church in Mill Run. During the 15-mile drive between the funeral home and the cemetery, Lydia could see her mother trying to be stoic, but her demeanor was crumbling like a stale cookie. The tears were rolling and her mother's chest began heaving as she tried to stifle her emotions. Noel was quick to grab her hand from across the fold-down armrests and tell her to just let it all out.

"This may not help, dear, but somewhere in Corinthians, it says that we are to not to fix our eyes on what is seen because it is temporary. Fix our eyes on what is unseen as it is eternal. Your father was such a good man and you know exactly where he is now," Noel told her.

Marilyn had no response but allowed a few more tears to fall before the procession stopped in front of the grave. Everyone exited the car and made their way up a small hill. Lydia noticed that the beautiful casket was now hanging from green straps above the freshly dug hole in the cold ground. When it was time to lower the coffin, Lydia peeked down the hole and saw a light colored concrete box. Randy told her it was called a vault. Her sister, Christy, locked arms on one side of Grandma and the other side with Marilyn as Lydia buried her face in Teddy's winter coat.

This is really it. No more Hinky Dinky songs, sitting in the matching rocking chairs, making sweet bread or sitting in church with him.

Now, as a woman approaching 50, what would Lydia say if she had the opportunity to have a real letter delivered to him? What would she say to let Grandpa Abe know what an influence he was on her early childhood? Perhaps it would go something like this:

Dear Grandpa,

First of all, I want you to know how much I miss you. That cold February that the stroke took your life, I was taken by surprise. I was old enough to understand that grandparents die, but I will always regret that I never got to say goodbye.

You must have known that I always felt an attachment to you that I never completely felt for Grandma or my grandparents on my dad's side of the family. As a child, I loved the calmness in your voice. Somehow it always carried wisdom too. I loved those hard-working hands of yours and admired what they must have been through being a farmer all of your life.

You always took Grandma's nagging with such grace. In my own marriage, I bark right back at my husband. How did you hold all of that in? There were so many other little things too. You were deep and wide like a river, deep in your patience and wide in your love for the earth and all of God's creatures. Do you know I hear your voice singing right next to me when I am in church and we sing hymns like "Blessed Assurance" and

Going Solo

"How Great Thou Art"? Instead of father time making things less painful, it still feels like you are right there holding my little hand and letting me run the pads of my fingers across your fingernails. I miss being in church with you.

The things I secretly teased you for or didn't understand I now find myself doing. I reuse a clean sheet of tin foil. I don't drink from plastic bottles. I try but often fail at holding my tongue with my husband, Vince. But most of all, Grandpa, I hope you are proud of my garden. When I garden each year, I do as much as possible in bare feet just to be connected to you and God's green earth. I remember that onions should be planted early or late but not in the heat of the summer. I always plant my tomatoes near basil to avoid those aphids and whiteflies. I put the pine shavings from our Christmas tree on the blueberry bushes to give the soil more acid. I can't remember all of the tips you taught me, but I remember the unconditional love and understanding that you gave to an energetic tom-boy who never knew when to shut up.

Thank you, Grandpa. Thank you for sending your spirit to me every time I pull a weed in the garden, hike in nature, cut up an old T-shirt for rags instead of using paper towels, drink from a spring, and take a spider outside instead of killing it. Thank you for the hymns I now call my own and secretly hope become my own children's favorites. Your spirit will always live on. You were a blessing to me.

Love, Lydia

CHAPTER FOUR

Montessori to Monticello

Lydia's Montessori School only went through the sixth grade. She left her class of six children, which was a combined class of fourth, fifth and sixth graders, to attend the public junior high school, Monticello. Cleveland Heights was such a diverse city, that it had everything from crummy, little bungalows near the next neighboring city to large mansions that would take your breath away. This imbalance of wealth frequently coincided with the racial demographics of Cleveland Heights. The city was continually redistricting the junior high schools to show egalitarianism.

Christy hated the public school experience and ended up at a private, all-girls school by the eighth grade. Teddy loved going to public school, but when it was Randy's turn, he hated public school for different reasons than Christy. She did not feel challenged there, while Randy was teased mercilessly for wearing nice clothes and carrying a briefcase. His chubbiness and effeminate qualities did nothing but get him beaten up. By eighth grade he too was attending private school, the all-boys school Noel had taught at for years. By the time Liddy was ready for junior high, the building where her siblings had started was torn down as the baby boomer population of the city began to decline. She ended up at the school that had the largest minority population.

Dad is so cool to let us all go to different schools. None of the teachers know my brothers or sister, so no one will expect me to be smart like them! Why on earth would Randy and Christy go to schools where they have to wear uniforms? There's no way I'd go to an all-girls school and have to wear a dress every day. Yuck.

Seventh grade ended up starting out horribly. Going from six well-behaved Montessori kids in a class to classes of 26 or more multicultural students was a bit of a shock for Liddy. She was teased for wearing the homemade clothing her grandmother had made, and she was the only one who did not ride the bus. Her father was used to taking the other kids to their respective schools, so driving was second nature to him. Maybe he was not even aware of the Monticello Junior High School bus pickup on the next block.

So many of the black girls were loud and talked so fast. They tended to hang out in groups. The white girls wore too much blue eyeshadow and tight jeans. They were so girlie and already knew each other from their elementary schools. It took her several weeks to find a single friend. It was a Jewish girl, very overweight and always talking about how she had been adopted. She was a chatterbox and often Lydia would tune out at her stories like Grandpa Abe must have done to her. She was also quite boy crazy and Lydia had no idea how she felt about the whole boy thing. Conversations in seventh grade went something like this:

"Do you think he likes me?" Debra would ask.

"I dunno. I think he likes you but not *likes* you likes you."

"Well, let's go to the Friday night skate and see if we'll see him there."

Friday Night Teen Skate was fun because Lydia actually knew how to skate.

Debra would just put her skates on and sit by the rink fireplace and flirt. Debra was always trying to fix Liddy up with some boy so that they could pair off and make out in the woods just beyond the parking lot. Liddy actually wanted to skate and had begged her parents for private skating lessons. Their family business was not always in the black, so that request often fell on deaf ears. Instead of flirting with boys, Liddy would use that time to imitate the girls in the middle of the ice doing their jumps and twirls.

The best part of Friday Night Teen Skate was that it was a profusion of what every junior high school kid was supposed to wear to survive. Nike, Levis, Daffy Dan's T-shirts with funny sayings on them, jean jackets, corduroys and Osh Kosh B'Gosh overalls. Eventually, Lydia prodded her parents into getting her the typical garb of the day except for the overalls. Marilyn insisted that in her day only poor farmers wore overalls to school and there was a stigma to wearing them in public.

Oh, my Goodness! No one is a farmer anymore. Why can't I be normal? I'll be like the only girl who doesn't have Osh Kosh.

Still, Lydia did her best to fit in and even began riding the school bus with Debra and the rest of the kids from the adjoining streets. Debra and Lydia were closer to Roxboro, another junior high school, but the racial redistricting made their middle school too far to walk to.

Most mornings she woke early to run with Noel before the walk to the school bus. Running was the special gift she and her dad had. None of the other kids in the family enjoyed sports. Christy was born with books in her hand, Teddy was always more interested in things that moved fast like cars and motorcycles, and Randy was born with bilateral clubbed feet. He never even learned to ride a bike until he was an adult and had to play a part in a play where he rode a bike across the stage. To further exacerbate his ankle problems, in high school he was in a car accident on the way to school and the oncoming car hit him in a way that shattered his right ankle. He lived many years with a metal pin and some screws keeping it all together. He joked about how he could tell when it was going to rain by the pain in his ankle.

Still thinking about her lack of overalls, Liddy was struck with an idea. She had raced several 10K races but was intrigued by her father's ability to run a full marathon. She made a deal with Noel that if she ran a full marathon, she could then *earn* a pair of overalls. Game on! They chose the marathon that ran from Buffalo, New York to Niagra Falls. Training would include occasional longer runs and an excuse to buy more running shoes. Both she and her father had more pairs of running shoes than most people had pairs of underwear.

The weekend soon arrived. How exciting it was to run right from Buffalo to Niagra Falls in Canada. The course went right over The Peace Bridge. Noel had a few marathons under his belt already, so he ran ahead to try to get a personal best. The finish line was slated to be taken down at the five-hour mark. Noel had finished before then, but he was too tired to go and run Liddy in. Her mother, who never ran, begged the race director to keep the finish line up for a few more minutes because her 13-year-old daughter was out there. He obliged her persuasiveness and Lydia finished at five hours 11 minutes. She earned her overalls, wore them about three times, then the trends changed and they were no longer cool!

Running became a unique time when Lydia and her father, Noel, could talk about problems at school, her latest crush, the next race they wanted to sign up for, and quite often they would talk about God. Noel had an exceptionally close relationship with Jesus. He considered Him to be his best friend. Liddy enjoyed hearing the stories of how her dad was a small child during the Great Depression and all of the crazy things that they had to do to survive.

Noel's father was an alcoholic as well as a skirt chaser. He tended to drink his paycheck and was not around much. Noel said that his best memory of his father was when he fell asleep in the mashed potatoes at Christmas dinner. Liddy could not even imagine any father figure other than Abe and Noel.

Noel and his older sister worked odd jobs, helped their mother financially when they could, and he even fished in Lake Erie for supper. He told one story about when he had not caught anything for the day. On his way home an older man who had quite a haul asked if he wanted one or two. "Yes, please," Noel replied, "but could you throw them to me so I can tell my mommy I caught them?" His honesty always impressed Lydia.

He told another story about how people in his neighborhood would go to the local diner and pour ketchup into the hot water pot meant for the tea. It made a great tomato soup when they didn't have enough money to buy a soup with their meal. The stories were never told to make Lydia feel sorry for Noel. They were always told in such a way that showed his fortitude and positive attitude toward the man he had become. He talked on and on about how he relied on Jesus and how he always knew that being a Christian was not a guarantee of an easy life, but the guarantee of a better life.

The struggles Lydia had fitting into Junior High had her chasing the next shiny object to find which clique she felt the safest with. She smoked her first cigarette in eighth grade and promptly threw up. She tried out for the track team but quit because she was scared of an older Italian girl who acted so tough all the time. The nerd group found her too immature and Lydia even tried pot while having a good run with the burnouts, but by the end of ninth grade, she ended up with her posse of a trio of boys. Dave C., Dave S. and Ricky. They actually *did* fun things. Dave S. was learning how to work on cars from his dad. Dave C. used an old lawnmower engine to make a go-cart and Ricky was just funny, always cracking people up.

As Lydia loved bike riding and was fit from running with her father, she never minded riding the four miles to the boys' houses, then all the way back to hang out on the strip called Coventry Yard by her home, and then back to the boys' homes to hang out some more. Being with your friends was no longer called playing. It was definitely *hanging out.*

Coventry Yard was a novelty for the Daves and Ricky. Lydia was proud to turn them onto a T-shirt shop called Daffy Dan's, and share the best milkshakes ever at a restaurant called Tommy's. Coventry was a crazy little strip with many small shops. It was like a tiny version of what she thought Haight-Ashbury must be like in California. Often there was a parade of freaks up and down the strip coming out of the head shop or playing hacky sack in front of the coffee house. The lesbians would hold hands coming out of the alternative bookstore and the Cleveland version of surfers would ride up and down the hill on their skateboards doing tricks off of the bike racks and curbs. Families would walk into the grocery store or over to the Coventry School playground. Bikers would congregate at the top of the hill near the movie theatre where each Saturday the theatre played *The Rocky Horror Picture Show*, attracting quite a cult following. Road racers would hang out at the bicycle shop purchasing skinny tire bikes and jerseys with pockets on the back.

Lydia and Dave C. became an item. It was exciting to have a boy she liked to kiss, and it didn't affect her hanging out with the other two boys, until it got closer to high school. David S. began poisoning David C. into thinking that when they all arrived at Cleveland Heights High School in the fall, he would not want to already have a girlfriend. There would be three Junior High Schools merging into one huge school and there would be many more women to pick from.

In eighth grade, Debra had encouraged Lydia to write in a diary like she always did. Since that time Lydia had burned through two of the small ones that had the tiny lock and key on them. So, by ninth grade, she had taken to writing in composition books her father had picked out for her from the local Revco drug store. The night of the breakup, she wrote:

I swear I'm going to punch David S. in the throat. Can't David C. make up his own damned mind? Who cares? Daddy and I are going to spend the summer getting Teddy to start running and quit smoking. I don't have to go to Pennsylvania for the summers anymore and Daddy says Teddy can start teaching me how to run the ABDick printing press. He even let me use his real camera which takes way better pictures than my Instamatic.

The balance of the summer before high school was spent running with Noel and sometimes Teddy, or sitting on her front porch talking to Debra about how stupid boys are, while Debra tried to convince her otherwise.

CHAPTER FIVE

The Five Year Disparity

With the trials and tribulations of junior high behind her, Lydia was looking forward to a fresh start at the only public high school in Cleveland Heights. Christy and Randy had stayed at their college preparatory private schools throughout high school, but Teddy loved public school and gave Lydia all sorts of advice about what to expect.

"And always come to me if anyone pulls any shit. No one is messin' with my kid sis."

"Thanks. I was thinking about that New School Program. Did they have that when you went?" she asked.

"Hell, my graduating class had about 1,200 people in it. That was nine years ago. They had so many options at the school that I really don't remember. Sorry, Liddy."

Next on her agenda was to get permission from her parents to sign up for New School. Rather than a traditional education, she begged her parents to allow her to sign up for this progressive program. The New Scholars were, to put it mildly, different. Nontraditional. Freethinkers. Out of the box. Maybe so far out of the box that they didn't even know there was a box type of thinkers. Although there were Harvard-bound kids in that program, most were not. Many signed up for New School to avoid the rigorous academics of the school. Maybe for Lydia, it was just a way to avoid the two Davids. Noel and Marilyn seemed very hesitant, so she had to shine brilliantly, convincing her parents that it was similar to Montessori.

"You guys liked the Montessori School, right?"

"Well, we liked the creativity and freedom, but sweetie we sometimes had to work with you over the summer to catch you up on more traditional learning," Mom said as delicately as she could.

This is B.S. They didn't catch me up. They carted me to Grandma's and let her force me to learn a bunch of futile garbage. I mean, gag me with a spoon!

"I read that they let you do things like running and skating as independent physical education. Mom, Dad, I don't want to do gym class where we hit each other with balls and run laps. I already run and it would give me more time to skate in the morning when I could do more patch time."

Lydia was beginning to skate patch time where the skaters had perfectly clean ice to practice school figures. She had gotten such a late start at official skating lessons and felt she had a lot of catching up to do. It was embarrassing learning jumps that 8-year-olds were also learning. She continued with her argument, "I can still go to the regular orchestra class, run cross country, see my other friends who are not in the New School Program and even get credit for taking classes outside of the school."

Both parents could see how unwavering she was on the subject and Noel always caved in when it came to his dear, sweet, little white rose. They signed off on the permission slips under the condition that she really would try to keep her grades up.

The Five Year Disparity

The Wednesday after Labor Day arrived and Noel stepped into the front yard to take a picture of Lydia and Debra, about to walk the two miles to their first day of high school. There was no school bus for the kids on Hampshire and the surrounding neighborhood. The busses were used for the kids coming from the neighboring city, University Heights. Lydia wore a Daffy Dan's T-shirt and light blue corduroy pants with an older pair of her running shoes. No backpack, no makeup, and no jewelry other than her multiple earrings. Simple and comfortable was her style, while boy-crazy Debra had plenty of makeup and a top with a bit of her cleavage hanging out enough to entice the other gender.

The walk was exciting. Lydia felt so grown up walking to high school. Debra wondered if she would be in any of the classes with the two Daves. Lydia knew that those two were not the New School type and knew she would not have any awkward moments seeing her old boyfriend and his buddy that broke them up. From their homes, they could have walked into the school through one of the back doors, but Debra insisted on walking all the way around the block to go in through the stately courtyard.

The High School was three stories tall and covered an entire block. Built in 1926 it was formidable and constructed to resemble a Tudor castle. It had a large clock tower that some mischief-makers had painted a Mickey Mouse on. The science wing was added in the 1960s when the school housed about 3,000 students. The location of the newer wing closed the courtyard off to the onlooking drivers traveling on Cedar Road. Trying hard not to be noticed, Lydia walked close to Debra until they were inside of the building. They parted ways as Debra found her homeroom and Lydia found the large open room on the second floor called New School.

For Lydia, the first three days of New School were a blast. The teachers preferred to be called by their first names, and the three-day orientation involved very little academics. Instead, there were games and activities to get to know each other. In one particular game, students formed into groups, then switched groups based on the criteria. To start, students were grouped by eye color. Next, by if they were born in Ohio or not, then what genre of movies they liked, by favorite color, and finally by age. When the age category was called out, most fell into the 16, 17 and 18-year-old groups, followed by a few 15-year-olds and only two 19-year-olds, Charlie and Ben. When the teacher, Fred, asked why Lydia had not yet found a group, she shyly stated that he had not yet called the 14-year-olds. She was it. Suddenly she wished that her November birthday would roll around quickly so that she would not be the only little kid in the New School Program.

When fun and games were over, she knew most of her classmates and found herself gravitating towards the oddballs of the group. Most of the people who attended the traditional part of the high school thought that *all* people who chose to attend the New School Program were oddballs. Because Lydia also played viola and ran cross country and track, she knew quite a few of the traditional high school students too, whom the New Scholars referred to as "truds." The "truds" would tease the New School Program by saying that they were in "No School," "Pre-School" or "Playschool."

What Lydia liked best about New School was the freedom. She did indeed get physical education credit for figure skating, running and juggling. She took an independent study and a student-led class. By the time she got to her senior year, she would spend only half a day there and take a bus down to Cleveland State to start college classes early. During the free period in high school, kids would congregate around a sort of common room with mechanical drawing tables and Berber carpeted blocks or they would hang out in the courtyard.

Liddy was approached by Charlie, one of the two 19-year-olds from orientation. He was emaciated and towered over her. He must have been 6 foot 2 and only weighed in at about 98 pounds. Liddy had at least 25 pounds on him at 5 foot 4. Charlie wore a cowboy hat to hide very thin hair. She learned that he had a sister one year younger than Liddy and he had an older brother who owned a bicycle shop on Coventry Road. His father was not in the picture and he never really talked much about his mother. Charlie was suffering from a rare blood disorder. He had bragged that his condition was so rare that he made it into three medical journals.

Her first reaction to Charlie was that he was weird. She also wondered what she had in common with a kid with a five-year disparity? Would her parents even let her hang out with someone that much older? Her parents were so protective of her and worried about boys since, besides the neighbor girl, Debra, they were all Liddy seemed to spend time with.

Lydia was torn between not wanting to be noticed and being noticed. As most teens, she wanted to fit into high school life. When Charlie would come up and make conversation with her or ask her if she wanted to hang out in the courtyard for her free period, she hoped that no one would assume that they were an item as they walked through the traditional part of the massive building.

When she and Dave had broken up at the end of summer, Noel had told her that living well was the best revenge. If that was true, then she wished she were walking down the hallways with a muscular, blonde, upperclassmen wearing a letterman jacket in case she bumped into one of the Daves, instead of this skinny guy with pasty skin, reddish hair and a cowboy hat.

As the first few weeks of school unfolded, she really began to enjoy Charlie's attention more and more. They would take their lunches out into the courtyard of the school and people-watch as they ate. The high school had an open campus during free periods and Cleveland Heights was one of the few cities in the 1970s where racial integration in the schools and neighborhoods seemed to be working. Watching the blacks, whites, Jews, hippies, burnouts, jocks, a few Asians and, of course, the preppies was so much fun. She knew that neither she nor Charlie quite fit into any particular mold.

"So why don't you have a boyfriend?" Charlie blurted out one day.

"I dunno. Boys are stupid."

"But that's all I ever see you with. Am I stupid?"

"Don't be silly. You're... you're Charlie. You're funny and nice and sweet like a brother."

Charlie looked down and Liddy could not see what his eyes were saying hidden from the brim of the cowboy hat. "So you could never see me as more than a friend?" he continued.

"I dunno. It's just that... Well, I dunno." She tried not to hurt his feelings. She didn't know what group she belonged in, but whatever it was or would be, she wanted to be well-liked and sought after. She had no idea what people thought about Charlie. He never seemed to talk about any other friends.

Oh my Gosh! He's so sweet but I couldn't see myself being his girlfriend. Why am I so shallow? What would it be like? He's always sick. I want someone who can skate and run and jump and stuff.

On the days that Charlie was back in the hospital, school seemed to drag on.

No wonder he is 19 and still has not finished high school! He is so smart but must have just missed too many days to graduate.

It was always a celebration when he returned and the day seemed a little bit more fun when she and her sidekick were together. Lydia walked over to her locker to throw her skating dress in and grab her viola case wedged in sideways. Charlie asked, "Did you go to homegroup today?"

Homegroup was the New School version of Homeroom. For the teachers, it was a time to take daily attendance, but for the students, it was a chance to have open discussions about things going on in the world around them before going off to their classes or lectures.

"No, I was at the skating rink for a figure lesson and my dad forgot to pick me up after his run. By the time I walked to the print shop to remind him, I was late. So, I guess no attendance for today. Wanna meet at the courtyard after I go to orchestra? I can't miss that."

"No, I've missed so much. Bob and Lou are teaching humanities class today so I'm gonna sit in on the lecture. Maybe go to my brother Ernie's bike shop after school?"

"Sure. Does he still have that silver Raleigh for sale?"

"Yep."

"See ya."

"See ya."

At the bike shop, Charlie's brother Ernie made cracks about Lydia's calf muscles. He too had very large calf muscles and claimed that Lydia actually had his beat by circumference. She should have been insulted. Girls her age should want to be skinny, blonde, demure, and have a nice rack. Lydia possessed none of those things and prided herself on her strength. She did not know many girls who could complete a full marathon at the age of 13. Lydia knew she was as strong as hell from running with her dad and was not bothered when boys or men made cracks about her strength. It was only when her girlfriends made those comments that made her feel fat and ugly. When around the male gender, she felt strong. Empowered. Appreciated. Tough. Solid. Invincible. Unconquerable.

Liddy walked over to the sleek racing bikes. She loved the drop bars on the speedy, lustrous, steel frames. One of them even looked like the red Masi that the character Dave rode in the movie "Breaking Away" that she and Teddy had just seen at the theater that month. She wanted the silver Raleigh racing bike to replace the junker she was riding. Long gone were the days of the pink bike with the streamers hanging off of the handlebars and the playing card rubbing against the spokes. She had been riding another junkyard bike Noel had pulled off of a tree lawn on garbage day. It was a Roadmaster and clunky as could be in an ugly shade of green. But there in the bike shop sat the most enticing, Raleigh Grand Prix ten-speed. It was the stylish design and all of those gear choices that stole her heart. She was already imagining her first bike race where she would magically beat all of the women and most of the men with her powerful thighs, working like engine pistons.

I wonder how many hours of collating and stapling I would have to do at the print shop to ride this baby.

Next, Lydia eyeballed the Vespa and Puch mopeds. It was the closest thing to one of Teddy's motorcycles she could get at age 14. Ernie saw the veritable drool coming from her mouth and he said, "Unfortunately, they all have governors on them. They will only go about 20 miles an hour even when you are pedaling too."

"But looking at your calf muscles," he continued, "I bet you would be the exception," he laughed.

Changing the subject, Lydia announced, "I'm ready for a Tommy's milkshake."

"I could eat," Charlie replied.

The two walked across the street and up the hill a short distance. Lydia signed in on the clipboard. Tommy's was frequently crowded and there was always a wait. While standing by the door, an older man with a yarmulke came in. He was slender and had a long, graying beard and strings called "Tzitzit" hanging from his coat. He went to sign in on the clipboard and his elbow rubbed Charlie's. As he turned to apologize, he called out "Charlie, my good friend!"

"Earl!" Charlie exclaimed.

"Why who is this?" he said with a hint of a New York accent.

"Earl Abromovitz, meet Lydia. Lydia, meet Earl Abromovitz."

The hostess announced Lydia's name, so Charlie hugged Earl and said they would catch up later. The two followed the hostess to an intimate booth on the north side of the restaurant. The 4-page laminated menus came but Charlie already knew what he wanted.

"Why do you always get the same thing when we eat here?" Lydia asked.

"My stomach is so sensitive that I know what will not make me sick later."

"Oh, I get it." But she really didn't get it. She could eat anything and outeat most of her family. Always trying to emulate her father, she even taught herself to adore dill pickles and bleu cheese salad dressing, two of his favorite things. When at Tommy's, she had a goal of eventually going through the whole menu by the time she was an adult. That was no small order, as Tommy always named his dishes after his regular customers and had an extensive menu of items named Aunt Gay, Keith, W. Zedd, Gordon, Mary Lynn and so on. Lydia chose a Bill Max, a Quigley and a mint chip milkshake. Life was just one new dish or two to scarf down.

As they were waiting for the food to materialize, Charlie explained how he had gotten to know Earl. He was a friend of his father's and often Charlie and Earl would have philosophical discussions about religion. He had not seen Earl in a long time and seemed excited to rekindle that friendship.

The milkshakes came and before taking his first sip, he looked Liddy square in the eyes and asked if he could take her to the movies.

"You mean like a date?" she responded.

"Well, yeah. Ernie can drive. No one trusts me behind the wheel."

"Umm," she stammered. "I guess I don't really think of you in that way. You're so cool, like my brother Teddy or something…"

The silence after that was palpable.

When the hell is that falafel coming? Why did he ask me that? He's nice and all but what will people think? It would be so weird. I'd have to stand on a chair just to kiss him goodnight. Just friends isn't so bad, is it? Didn't we just have this conversation in the courtyard a while ago?

The meals finally arrived and were served with the best pita bread and side of hummus this side of the Middle East. The fries were to-die-for and Lydia poured hot sauce on them and started shoveling them in her mouth hoping that her constant chewing would stave off having to answer any more awkward questions.

Many outings took place over the next few months. Most were with Charlie and at least one other boy, or once in a while, a girl as a buffer. One evening the plan was to all go Dutch to the Magic Pan Restaurant. Lydia had her money tucked inside her pants pocket but Charlie not only had carnations for her but also did not let her pay. Since the drinking age was younger at that time, he was old enough to order wine. Liddy felt so grown up eating out with the guys and sipping wine.

The days got colder as the North Coast always does. Courtyard people-watching and trips to Coventry Yard turned into staying in the New School area where students could stretch out on the carpeted blocks and do schoolwork on the drafting tables. Once in a while, students from the traditional part of the school would also come into the New School common area during their free period. Lydia had become friends with one of these "truds" and invited Aaron over to meet Charlie. About the only thing they had in common was their height. Aaron dressed flamboyantly and Charlie favored the same old jeans and flannel shirt. Aaron made jokes about his Jewish heritage while Charlie was searching for some sort of relationship with a higher power and took it quite seriously. The one thing they had in common besides being tall and slim was Lydia.

When Aaron went to his next class and Lydia was alone with Charlie they got into some interesting conversations about God. Lydia wondered if he was struggling with his illness and may not make it to see marriage and kids. He often brought up faith or lack of it in his family and really wanted to attend some kind of church. He said he had gone to a church in his neighborhood one time.

"I went alone and brought a Bible with me. I swear the people were so fake. Someone teased me about my Bible. I guess it wasn't the right one or something. Is there more than one kind of Bible?" he asked one day.

The sad thing was, Lydia loved God and loved the way her dad always talked about Jesus but she had not yet had her own "come to Jesus" moment and she felt uncomfortable sharing her love for God. She was still worried about being popular and reluctant to invite Charlie to church with her. Still, her heart ached for her friend and she wondered if talking to his friend Earl, the Jewish man, would help in some way.

She was also reluctant to invite Charlie to her church because it was in downtown Cleveland. No one from her group of friends or neighborhood attended. It must have been a grand church at one time when Euclid Avenue was called Millionaires' Row and the area was not so sketchy. Now the majority of the congregation came down from the suburbs and her own mother said that most of the congregation was a bunch of blue bloods or old wealth. Well, she had surely gotten the "old" part correct. There were only four or five kids in Lydia's confirmation class. She just could not see Charlie getting much out of her church.

Should I invite him? That would be so weird. What do I say? I'm like 15. What the hell do I know about being saved or going to heaven? Would Dad and Mom think we are dating? Why doesn't his family take him to church? Are they atheists?

The questions were buzzing in her head as she tried to talk about what her faith meant to her.

"Well, I've just always gone to church. I guess I take for granted that it's what you're supposed to do on Sunday. My church is a bunch of old people, but it's where my mom and dad met. It's also where my dad was baptized when dinosaurs roamed the earth," Liddy teased.

"So do you think we all get a chance to go to heaven?"

"Gosh, I hope so."

" I guess what doesn't seem fair is that the Bible says that every tribe and nation has to hear the word of God before Jesus can return. What about all the people on some weird island that we have not even discovered yet? How do they get to learn about God? What if I don't figure this out in time?"

In time for what? Is he dying? Does he think he has to figure it all out now?

These were thought-provoking questions to be sure. She was flattered that he was confiding in her but she felt so powerless about sharing what she knew. She could not recite Bible verses like her father could. She could not tell the difference between what the Old Testament said to do and what the New Testament freed you up to do. All Lydia knew was the feeling of profound love in her heart when she sat in the huge sanctuary of her church. She knew God was there. She also knew He was there when she and Dad were running side by side at 6:30 in the morning, when the pinkish clouds gave way to the morning sun. She knew God was there when she saw a cardinal, pecking at the seeds in the birdhouse at her grandparents' home. She knew He was there when her parents fell in love. She knew that someday God would be there for her when she needed Him to be, but for now, she took the whole God thing for granted. She often treated God like a Pez dispenser, only praying to him when she needed a good grade on a test or when she wanted to win her event at a track meet and, like that Pez dispenser, she expected her results to pop right out like a little, rectangular confection.

CHAPTER SIX

There are Mormons at the Door

Over the next couple of days, Charlie continued his quest for knowledge and found that the Mormon faith really excited him. He must have had some Mormon missionaries come to his door and he was so hungry to believe in something that their enthusiasm hooked him, line and sinker like a starving trout. He wanted to know if the elders could come over to Lydia's house and talk. He was afraid of what his family would think if they did their sales pitch at his home.

"Um, I dunno. I guess I could ask my dad," she replied.

"That would be great. There is this bishop named Bishop Gayle and two elders who spoke with me last week."

Lydia's brother Randy was around when Lydia asked her dad if the elders could come and talk one evening. "Oh, is his name Barry?" Randy asked and then cracked up laughing saying "elderberry, Elder Barry! Ha Ha."

Noel reprimanded him and said that he would allow it. Lydia began riddling off questions about what was so different about the Mormon faith and theirs. "I guess we will find out when they come," Noel replied.

The next evening Noel made sure that if Randy was around, he would be respectful. When the doorbell rang, Noel led two men, Charlie and Lydia to their dining room table. The missionaries talked about the Bible being only one book, but that they also used the Book of Mormon. This book came from gold plates located in New York back in 1820. It sounded strange that a man had a dream or vision to go and dig up some plates and try to figure out what they meant. She had always heard that Mormons could have more than one wife and that they considered the Holy Trinity to be three separate Gods. They spoke and Lydia could see that Charlie was hooked. He was so excited to feel loved by someone who seemed to have all the answers. After Noel escorted the three of them out he sat with Lydia at the table and asked what she thought.

Lydia started with, "Well, it's cool that Charlie has a faith in something I guess, but how did this Joseph Smith find the scrolls or plates or whatever in some mountain in New York? Doesn't it seem like he was just copying what Moses from the Old Testament did when he went up the mountain to get the 10 commandments?"

"It does sound strange, but I suppose no more strange than Jonah being swallowed by a whale. I know this must be hard for you to be baptized as a United Methodist, have a Baptist mother and grandmother and have spent six years at a Jewish Montessori, but I can assure you my dear, that God is God, one and only. We try to put labels like Baptist, Episcopalian, Catholic and so on to these beliefs. But truly we should be focussed on the *relationship* and not the *religion*," Noel assured her.

"So Charlie wants to be Baptized. Isn't he too old?"

"Baptism is a public declaration of your faith in God. There is no age limit. When we baptized you, you were only a baby and could not make that decision for yourself, but it was a way for me and your mother and the whole church congregation to promise to raise you in the faith of our Lord, Jesus Christ. We hope that you will, or already have, made that decision in your own heart to love God with all your heart," he finished.

Lydia had a lot to think about that night. She wanted to support Charlie but thought that it was a weird way to share your faith. Would he have to dress in a suit and knock on people's doors and try to convert them? Would he be the next Mormon at the door? She laughed thinking of him in a suit with his cowboy hat on.

New School had an ice skating night and Lydia was pumped to show off all of her skills. She had been doing school figures and freestyle sessions in the morning before school as part of her physical education requirement to graduate. As much as she said she did not want to go out with Charlie as a boyfriend-girlfriend thing, she could not wait to show off to him. He was ill that night and unable to attend. He was sorely missed. Maybe she should not have been so quick to judge his appearance and illness.

Charlie did graduate that year and during the summer there were a few times that she and Aaron visited him or talked to him on the phone. He had made another trip to and from the hospital, so she and Aaron picked out a Hallmark card and a plant to deliver to him. They assumed that if he was out of the hospital he must be doing well. That was not the case. On a sunny afternoon in August, Lydia was at the print shop when Earl Abromovitz called to tell Marilyn that Charlie passed away. Not knowing exactly what to say, Lydia left the front office of the print shop to cogitate on this news. She walked home feeling numb and empty. Later that same evening, Bishop Gayle called Lydia at her home and asked if she would say something at his funeral. Her first an immediate reaction was "no." The Bishop was kind and made her feel like she was one of his closest friends and that Charlie often spoke about her.

"Please reconsider. I will call again," he said.

When she did agree, she spent the next two days in complete anguish over what exactly to say. Her mother, Marilyn, told her to write it out on index cards that she would bring home from the print shop. Her father told her to just speak from the heart.

On the day of the funeral, Lydia made herself wear a dress. It was a simple print with three-quarter-length sleeves and rode just above her knees. Her father drove her to The Church of Jesus Christ of Latter-Day Saints. Arriving a full hour early, she still had nothing written for the eulogy. Scribbling some thoughts on one of the cards, she sat toward the front. At the designated time, she approached the pulpit. She placed her card down on the lectern and stared out at all of those faces. They were all staring back at her. Her mouth was so dry that if she opened it, her lips would stick to her teeth. She wasn't a writer. She was still in disbelief that he was really gone. This was different than her grandfather passing. He was old. Charlie had not yet even gotten to kiss a girl. He had wanted to kiss her, but she always told him she thought of him as more of a brother. Ouch. That must have hurt. Licking her lips once, she said a few words about how kind he was and how he always made everyone feel important. That was all she had in her before the wave of tears began gushing down her cheeks. Red-faced and embarrassed she ran back to her seat and hoped that people understood.

Lydia blocked the rest of the day from her memory. Did her father stay and take her home or did she get a ride from a friend? Did she talk to Earl, Ernie and Charlie's mom? She must have. Her memory of that day was put into some deep, dark place that she never wanted to visit again.

There are Mormons at the Door

Dear Charlie,

This is only my second letter to a dead man, so forgive me for any awkwardness in expressing my joy at knowing you and being your friend. I may ramble and flounder a bit, as more than 30 years have passed since our time together.

In high school, I was a real jerk. I lived inside of a little Lydia bubble that had a circumference of only about two feet. It was my little, safe world. I only saw what I wanted to see and tried so hard to be popular and liked by what I assumed were the "cool" kids. Little did I know then, you were one of the coolest kids ever.

You wore a Texas, cowboy hat... in Cleveland! Who does that? You were so smart but never smug. You were funny but never tried to steal the show. You were an amazing friend and would drop everything for me yet you never asked me to rescue you.

I had no idea how strong your romantic feelings may have been for me. Well, maybe I did but I quickly dismissed them waiting for something I deemed would be better. Stupid me. I will always regret that. Perhaps it was your illness and physical appearance that made me nervous when you would try to make a move on me, but that was not on you, Charlie. That was my own insecurity and my own hang up. What a superficial buffoon I was. I apologize.

I was so self-absorbed that I had no idea what you were truly going through being poked and prodded at the doctors and the pain some of the treatments must have caused you. I was just trying to be a normal teenager, but so were you! As I have recently finished raising my own three teenagers, I feel like a fraud when I worked avidly to teach them not to judge, yet I judged. I taught them not to feel entitled, and to love everyone equally, but did I love you equally?

Letters to the Dead Men

I want to formally apologize for not being the kind of friend you may have needed me to be during those last months of being in your physical body. I pray that you are free from pain, happy, fulfilled and well-loved on the other side of this physical experience. Charlie, I love you.

Love, Lydia

CHAPTER SEVEN

Filling the Void

Eleventh grade for Lydia started out well. Whenever she saw Charlie's old locker, she just remembered that he had graduated and that was why it was now being occupied by a kid with greasy, brown hair and the beginning of a man-beard. She did not think about the fact that he should have been in college, learning something brilliant and dazzling some other girl with his charm.

She had passed another figure skating test at the end of summer and began her cross country season well. Her free periods were spent in the courtyard of the school or in the New School common room, which was now becoming a refuge for more of the "truds" who were cutting class. Aaron was one such frequent class-cutter who hid out in there. This year he seemed even more effeminate and animated than he was over the summer. He was as funny as the day was long and although he liked top 40 music, he was always introducing Liddy to new music that had not yet hit the top 40. They danced around the common room singing the lyrics to "Rock Lobster" and "Private Idaho" from the B52's.

They made strange, red paper hats to dance to imitating the "Whip It" song by Devo.

Aaron also had a serious side. He and Lydia adored the artists of Carly Simon and Joni Mitchel with their sad love ballads. They spent hours on Coventry Road at Record Revolution, the record store that had hundreds of new and used vinyl records to complete their collections.

Lydia had a major crush on Aaron, even though her "gaydar" was exceptional, having suspected for years that her own brother, Randy, was gay. She decided to bring up Randy one time to test the waters of what Aaron would say. He claimed he was straight, yet she never knew of a straight guy who looked like he stepped off of the cover of a GQ magazine. She and Aaron had kissed a few times, but she knew she was not going to convert him. She saw the irony in her company with Aaron. He didn't want to kiss her any more than she wanted to kiss Charlie. Still, he helped fill the void of Charlie's absence.

Aaron brought out a wild and reckless side of Liddy she never knew she had. Often times Aaron would borrow his dad's 1972 Vista Cruiser full on with the hideous, fake wood panels down the side and lots of rust. They picked up Aaron's friend Roger and drove to a wealthy suburb not far from the Heights. The three snuck into a country club across from the mall in Beachwood. Leaving their clothes by a sandpit, they went streaking all over the golf course. Aaron's favorite thing to do was to lie flat on his front and leave a reverse snow angel in the sand for the golfers to see in the morning. They all giggled thinking about what the golfers would think when they saw the frontal imprint in the sand the next morning.

"You do it too Liddy. Leave your boobs print in the sand."

"Aaron, there's another sand pit farther down. Let's go," Roger encouraged.

Lydia, being the better runner of the three, kept up with the boys with ease.

Other nights she would drive her 1976 Dodge Omni to Aaron's home and just listen to albums while he played dress up. Lydia would take pictures of him with her father's Nikon 35 mm camera. Aaron talked about his very weird relationship with his father and how close he and his mother were. Liddy talked more about her gay brother and how he too was a momma's boy.

"Randy and I just never got along," she proclaimed. "I mean, he always uses big words like he is better than I am. I get that my dad was an English teacher for a long time so we all have a decent vocabulary, but he would say shit like 'You impudent shrew' when he was mad at me. One time he called me a skunked breathed Leviathan. I don't even know what a Leviathan is!" She continued, "When I was little he used to take my wrist and make me hit myself while saying 'Why are you hitting yourself?' He would lick his finger and wipe it on me and say 'Lilac' then I was supposed to go and lick my finger, wipe it on him and say 'Honeysuckle,' but his arms were longer and I could never get him back."

"I have an older brother too. They suck. Thankfully mine moved out so all I have is my little brother who is a total putz. And my dad basically ignores me because I am not normal."

"What does that mean?"

"I dunno!"

"Well, I know, but I remember that my parents didn't know for a long time about my brother Randy, but they found out one summer when I was at my grandparents."

"How did that go?" he asked.

"From what I heard, not great at first. Randy was sick and in bed. Dad had gone running in the morning and saw a *Scene Magazine* while doing his cool down walk on Coventry. Randy and some friends were on the cover of the magazine and it was a story about gays."

"Woa. Did he freak out?" Aaron was at the edge of the bed eager to hear more.

"Well, yes. He came home and he and showed my mom. They went up to his room to bring him a pitcher of water and they asked him about it. When he came clean and said he was gay, my Mom just screamed 'No, you're not!' and she dropped the pitcher and started digging through his drawers to look for drugs that made him gay. Hysterical!" Lydia said.

"Drugs? Seriously?" he said, laughing.

"Well, dad calmed her down and I guess talked to Randy afterward. For a super long time I think they were in shock, but now they seem okay and even used his boyfriend to help out at the print shop when we had a rush order to get out." Lydia continued: "My dad is all about Jesus and he says we are not supposed to judge. That's God's job. We talked about it on one of our runs when I came back from my grandparents. He told me that we should not love the lifestyle, but love the person."

"Cool"

Eager to change the subject, Aaron asked "What's your curfew?"

"12, why?"

"'Cuz I want us to go and see *The Rocky Horror Picture Show* sometime. I heard you were a Rocky Horror virgin. Are you in?"

"I'll see."

All Liddy knew of *The Rocky Horror Picture Show* was that it was a movie with a cult following. Aaron had seen it several times but Liddy wasn't sure if she could figure out a way to sleep at Debra's or sneak home late. The movie started at 11 p.m. and even though it was right on Coventry Road, a half mile from her cozy home, she would still miss curfew.

"Wanna see my Bar Mitzvah pictures? We went to Israel," Aaron said as he hopped off of the mattress and went to a shelf by his bed.

"Sure"

The pictures told a thousand words. Aaron's dad was always bored or taking the photo, while the mom and Aaron were always laughing and holding hands or standing next to each other. The two brothers appeared in the pictures as ordinary as possible, with their expressions rather humdrum. Aaron was surely the one who got all of the attention with his outwardly gregarious personality. And yet, maybe he was lonely for his dad's attention. The pictures just made her feel sad for him somehow.

As she drove home that evening, she pondered more on what *normal* really meant.

That evening she pulled out her journal and poured out her heart. It read: *I really don't understand myself. Who am I? When I used to race and beat the boys back at Montessori I got teased. The girls would chant "Liddy the Lez.. Liddy the Lez." I had to come home and ask Randy what a lez was. I was grossed out when he said it was when girls kissed girls. Junior high school sucked for the most part because I thought I would get a fresh start going from Montessori to public school. But junior high was what Daddy called "culture shock" going from a small private school to a diverse, public school. I couldn't stand the prissy girls who obsessed over make-up and fashion. They read* Teen Magazine *and* Tiger Beat *for Christ sake! Who cares about that crud? Give me a T-shirt, pair of Levis and some Nikes and I'm good to go. I like boys and thought I even loved David in 9th grade. When he dumped me I didn't give up on boys. But now in high school, I have all of these unusual friends or gay or bisexual friends like Aaron and Roger. So now instead of the girls telling me, I am a "lez" Debra says they are calling me "fag tag" and "fag hag" behind my back. Why can't I just be me and like who I like and still have some normal boys like me back?*

After placing the diary in the back of her closet, under her track shoes, she got into bed and stared up at the underside of the canopy bed that used to belong to her sister, Christy. Lydia hung little ornaments and pins on the metal rods that held the fabric in place. She stared at the colorful strings and things she placed on there until she drifted off to dreamland.

When the next weekend rolled around Liddy called Aaron and Roger to see if they were going to go to the movies or out to eat. This unusual three-way date was usually implied unless otherwise talked about during the school week. They chose to drive around the mall parking lot in the Vista Cruiser until the car rolled over to 100,000 miles. It was precariously close to rolling over, so they thought it would be fun to watch the old dial go from 99,999 to 100,000. It was much more exciting to see then before the dials all became digital. The three were belting out the lyrics to "Young Blood" by Rickie Lee Jones. "Two for a movie show, three in the back row, hold on tight! Remember, you might have looked like cool twelve but your fuse felt just like dynamite." They sang and laughed and realized that when they looked at the odometer, they had missed it: 100,000.4

No worries. They were off to McDonald's for some green, shamrock shakes. Liddy took turns taking pictures of Aaron and Roger spewing the shakes across the parking lot, in their very best impersonation of Linda Blair spitting up green pea soup in the 1973 movie *The Exorcist.* Aaron had Liddy home by 11 and Roger home soon after so that they could all be in front of their TV sets for *Saturday Night Live* at 11:30. If one of the three missed it, the shame they would endure at school on Monday was just not worth it. On this night the Ohio punk rock band "Devo" was the musical guest. No one wanted to miss that!

True to his word, Aaron and Lydia did eventually go to Coventry to see *The Rocky Horror Picture Show* for her first and his 20th time. Although they did not dress up like many of the other obsessives, Aaron did throw toast, get up and dance to the "Time Warp" and shout out that they would be having meatloaf for dinner. Lydia watched the audience as much as she watched the screen as she was in wonder at the length that people went to memorizing lines and doing hair, makeup and costume.

Roger, Aaron, Liddy and a new member of the gang, John, began spending more and more time together. John was a bit on the nerdy side, and had wild, thick blonde hair. He had a girlfriend, yet seemed to like being part of this new foursome. Everyone except Roger had a car and driving privileges, so someone was always able to pick up the other members and get pizza, see a movie, go to one of the other's houses to listen to music or have deep conversations. Somehow those conversations always seemed to be about sex or the lack of it. It was a confusing time for Liddy as Roger was the only one who was proudly flaunting his sexual orientation. Aaron claimed he still liked girls and John kept trying to sneak kisses to Lydia when the other boys were not around. One night it was just too much. Out came the diary.

Good God! How do I express these feelings of mine? I feel so completely alone and yet I am surrounded by people. I can't figure it out. I don't think I love Aaron, although I like him a lot. Somehow I feel as if I am a total alien to this whole world. Nothing belongs to me anymore. I am just an observer and that's a lousy feeling. Aaron can be so sweet, but tonight he was so mean. When we were talking about stuff, he dragged me over to a mirror and said "Look at yourself. You are in baggy pants and a running shirt and a ponytail. You want to make out with me but I am afraid that if I go any farther, I might find out you're a dude!" That was the most hurtful thing I have ever heard him say to me. Thank goodness Roger jumped in and ragged on Aaron about what a jerk he was being. I think Aaron is just an ass because he won't admit that he really is gay. He should just come out already! And then what's up with John? He keeps trying to kiss me and I thought he had a girlfriend already. Why isn't he out with her?

Soon after that diary entry, Aaron decided that he had better come clean with his friends. No one was shocked and Roger just claimed "Finally!" Lydia's brother Randy snuck Aaron and Liddy into a gay restaurant/bar in downtown Cleveland one night. She knew she could never have anything but a platonic relationship with Aaron, but she still remembered his soft lips the few times that they had kissed. When Randy and Aaron started flirting with each other, she tried to swallow before the bile started to rise in her throat. At age 16, she still grappled with what God thought of the gay lifestyle and tried not to think about what parts go where in a gay relationship. It still did not seem anatomically appropriate to her.

A Donna Summers song came on and both boys grabbed spoons to use as microphones from the booth where they were all sitting. They sat on the table and belted out the lyrics about the cake in MacArthur Park getting rained on. Watching the two flamboyant performances made Liddy smile. She admired how they seemed at peace being in a place where they were free to be who they really were. Did she ever feel like she was who she wanted to be in her racing T-shirts, baggy pants and running shoes? Yes. She loved being draped over a bicycle or up to her elbows in grease working in the garage while her other brother Teddy worked on a car. But very few people understood her the way she had hoped they would. They made judgments.

The next song broke her reverie, the always popular Village People song "Y.M.C.A." Aaron grabbed Liddy and pulled her out onto the dance floor. He started doing all of the letters with his arms and legs. Lydia never enjoyed dancing or anything she considered "girlie." She quickly tried to hide behind the other dancers and awkwardly slipped back to their booth as quickly as possible. Her fear of being a poor dancer was not as bad as the fear that people seeing her in this bar would think that she was gay too. It sure seemed plausible. She had on her baggy Forenza pants that later were called M.C. Hammer pants. She had on high-topped sneakers that were barely tied. Her T-shirt boasted of her latest 10K running race. The only thing she needed to look like the stereotype of the day would be a flannel shirt!

And so the questions began in her head so similar to the ones she had recently written in her journal. Where did she fit in? Could she be gay? She did have 16 piercings in her ears. That was "girlie," wasn't it? But it was also a bit bad-ass. She dreamed of owning her own motorcycle like Teddy yet she liked kissing boys. Most of her male friends were just that. Friends. She wasn't particularly attracted to girls. The only time she looked at them was to see if they were prettier than she was or more slender than she was. She still cared about her appearance, but just didn't see the point in all of that glop they put on their faces.

A poem came to her head from a record her father had purchased for her back in the days of Montessori. It was from the Marlo Thomas record called *Free To Be You and Me.* The record was a smash and sold over 500,000 copies. Her father always bragged about being a feminist before it was popular. Since he had a raging alcoholic father, he was truly raised by his two favorite women, his mother, and his big sister, Norine. He loved and respected strong women. Noel and Liddy listened to this album hundreds of times and now the poem came back to reassure her.

My Dog is a Plumber by Dan Greenburg*

My dog is a plumber. He must be a boy,
Although I must tell you his favorite toy
Is a little play stove with pans and with pots,
Which he really must like, 'cause he plays with it lots,
So perhaps he's a girl -- which kind of makes sense,
Since he can't throw a ball and he can't climb a fence,
But neither can dad -- and I know he's a man,
And mom is a woman and she drives a van.
Maybe the problem is in trying to tell
Just what someone is by what she does well?

Lydia laughed silently and stopped worrying as she, Randy and Aaron made their way out of the bar and back into Randy's car. The ride home was uneventful. It was late and Lydia was known for falling asleep as soon as activity stopped. She had already gone for a run, had a full day of school and even snuck in a freestyle ice skating session before they had gone out. Now it was late. Her legs felt like lead and she knew she would be running with Noel and possibly Teddy in the morning.

CHAPTER EIGHT

Best of Show

Senior year of high school had the potential of being fun for Lydia. With most of her credits needed to graduate completed by the end of her junior year, she had time to stay at the ice skating rink all morning and work on her program for an upcoming test session. She began each morning with 45 minutes of figure eights followed by 45 minutes of freestyle skating. If she was running late she would throw her jeans and shirt on over her skating dress (the only time she ever enjoyed wearing a dress) and drive her Dodge Omni to school in time for orchestra. She no longer had to race to the print shop and bother her father for a ride. She stunk at the viola from lack of practice and the inability to sit still long enough to play well. Still, there were only four who played the viola and her orchestra needed everyone's participation.

With a quick change in the bathroom to remove her skating dress, she went off to the humanities class Charlie had loved so much. It was taught by a teacher with rather severe cerebral palsy. She had to pay attention or she would not be able to decipher his difficult speech. She liked the class because it opened her up to new ideas and it made her think on a whole new level. She stayed in the back of the class, though, as there were a few kids in the class who truly annoyed her. One was a girl who always bragged about how she had never been so intellectually stimulated in a class and wanted to be a lobbyist in Washington, D.C.

What a kiss ass! Who goes up to a teacher and sucks up that much? What the hell does a lobbyist do anyway? And that guy she always hangs out with. What a pretentious ass. They hang on every word Bob says and take crazy ass notes. Why? It's not like Bob grades hard. All we have to do is write opinion papers and we'll pass.

Three days a week she parked the car at the print shop and took the Regional Transit downtown to begin taking freshman level classes at Cleveland State University, so her time with Aaron became less frequent but still meaningful. The other two school days she would try to find Roger and Aaron in the cafeteria. Finding them, she slid her tray over to Aaron, as a girl from her junior high days sat on his other side.

Geez! I have gotten so out of touch with people. JoEllen and I used to be sort of close at Monticello and we hung around the same group of people. Now she has become the biggest debutante. Her hair ribbon matched her belt and her Izod shirt matched her socks. She talked like such a "Gidget" about how great our senior year is going to be. Maybe hers will be, but I am not so sure about mine. Is hanging around Aaron and Roger the whole year all I'm in for?

Lydia always helped out at the print shop but also began working at the skating rink handing out skates and being a safety guard. During one of the adult skating sessions, a party boy and his buddies were fairly drunk and wanted to see what it was like to skate inebriated. He was blonde, had broad shoulders and rosy cheeks. His deep brown eyes caught her attention and she enjoyed flirting with him. Six years older that Liddy, Matt was her brother Randy's age. She didn't think Matt would ever ask her out, but she could not help skating over to him to see how drunk he really was and then chatting with him until the end of the session.

He did ask her out a few weeks later and because of the age difference, she wasn't sure how to approach asking for her parents' permission to see an older man. She assumed that keeping their budding romance hidden for a while couldn't hurt. She chose to test the waters of her omission of truth by asking strange questions of her father on their morning runs.

"So how much older are you than mom?" she asked one morning.

"I'm about four years older."

"Is that why Grandma never liked you? Did she think you were too old or something?"

"Well, I suppose that had something to do with it, but I think more than that, she only had one child. No one would ever be good enough for her little princess. Plus, they grew up in the sticks of southern Pennsylvania. I doubt your Grandma ever made it any farther than Maryland or West Virginia. Letting her only baby go off to college in a big city like Cleveland must have been difficult. I let her animosity towards me go a long time ago." He continued, "Did I ever tell you how your mom and I met?"

"Yeah, like a million times! You met in the church choir."

"Well, not exactly. I was singing in the church choir with my sister, Norine. Marilyn attended church with her uncle who lived in the area. In those days ladies were usually accompanied by a gentleman. Man, did I fall hard for those blue eyes and fiery, red hair. I could barely sing watching her in one of the front rows as I was up on the chancel. The problem was, I assumed that her uncle was her husband. Maybe she had married an older man. Funny thing was, she would always see me with my sister and assume that Norine was my girlfriend. She had been attending Epworth Euclid U.M.C. ever since she started college at Mather, and it must have been about three months before someone told me that the older guy was her uncle."

Noel and Lydia rounded the corner of a side street heading onto Fairmount Boulevard where his sister Norine lived, and she was too out of breath to ask him much more.

Teddy knew about Lydia sneaking around with her new beau, and he also knew that such beau drank alcohol as well as used drugs. He was leery of this boy's attention. "I've seen him at the bars, Lydia. He's a drinker. I mean, not just casual. I may have even seen him do a line or two," he said one day when they were working at the print shop.

"I'll watch it. You know I would never try cocaine, Teddy!"

"Still, you hang around with dogs and you are gonna get fleas."

"I get it."

"Liddy, I'm serious! I don't know this guy. I'm not saying I don't trust him, but if you ever do anything like coke or stuff, you had better tell me. I want to know where he gets his shit from. I know some dealers lace their snow will all sorts of crap just to make a buck," he told her.

"Yeah, okay," she assured him, even though she was deathly afraid to try anything harder than pot.

That night her diary entry was all about how sweet it was that Teddy was so concerned for her. *Geez! Why would I want to do hard drugs? I am terrified that once it's in you, and you realize that you are too high, you can't do anything about it. At least when I smoked pot at Monticello, I could just stop when I felt silly. I don't think Matt would ever pressure me into doing coke with him. All I know is that I'm going to try to only see him as little as possible. He scares me with how good of a kisser he is. It's like he has this power over me and I am scared we will start doing stuff I can't stop. And I'm NOT talking about the drugs!*

Eventually, her parents found out about Matt. The phone calls Lydia got were quite obviously from a boy, and they knew she didn't talk to Aaron or Roger like that. Matt had dropped out of college at Cleveland State University and had found a full-time job. With his job and party friends, he didn't have a lot of time for her in the beginning. There was no pressure to become exclusive so Lydia still hung out with many of her New School friends.

Lydia kept her Matt world separate from her Aaron and Roger world. She barely ever talked to Matt about anything pertaining to high school because she assumed he wouldn't care about such baby stuff, being a grown man with a job. They listened to mainstream rock and went to bars that did not carefully check her ID. When she was with him she thought that Aaron and Roger were too silly to be adults. She acted older, or what she thought was more sophisticated or mature. Yet, when with Aaron and Roger, she did weird things like play dress up, take pictures of their escapades, streak, listen to college radio and alternative music and laugh at the craziest things while sitting on swings at the playground. To top it off, she still had her morning runs with her father when they would talk about God, family, morals and future goals. She was asking a lot of herself, playing these three different roles all of the time, which was one of the reasons she enjoyed being with Teddy so much.

Teddy knew her for who she wanted to be that day and he just loved the hell out of her, no matter her mood. At the print shop, if there was a rush order coming in, Teddy would print the book, catalog or pamphlet, and then the whole family would stay late collating and stapling it. They counted out the sets to make sure there were enough printed and then order pizza. Teddy and his girlfriend Sue had created a funny language and had all sorts of words they used instead of the usual words. He let Liddy in on their funny language and she felt privileged. Sue treated her like a cool little sister too and Liddy hoped Sue and Teddy would marry someday.

Lydia loved how Teddy was always asking about Matt and watching over her relationship with him. She knew he only wanted the best for his kid sis. Teddy had not gone to college right out of high school and now in his mid-20s had just signed up for classes at the community college to learn how to shoot and edit film. He wanted to marry Sue and they had talked about it, but

Sue didn't seem as ready as Teddy to settle down. Still, Lydia had heard from Randy that Teddy was squirreling away money for a ring. It was the best secret she ever kept. She giggled every time she saw Sue and Teddy together.

Noel was still trying to get Teddy to keep running with him during those early mornings. Teddy was not a morning person and had only done a few dozen runs with them over the years. There was no consistency perhaps because of the cigarettes. The only thing those occasional runs did for Teddy was to make him want to quit smoking.

"Man, after I run, I can't smoke for like two hours," he commented one day. "It's like my lungs are on fire. Geez! Liddy, you and dad were kicking my butt." Lydia blushed with his compliment and was excited to think that he may quit smoking because of her and Noel's influence. She winced remembering the cigarette she tried in eighth grade.

Around the time of the great running experiment, Teddy began working on a chopper motorcycle. It was a Triumph and had no front brakes. Teddy, a small man of no more than 165 pounds, had to practically stand up on the bike to get the rear brake to stop the momentum when he rode fast. That bike was a thing of beauty. Purchased used, in need of much help, it kept him busy for hours and hours in the garage. He had long since moved out of the Hampshire house, but still used the large garage for all of his repairs and fix up jobs. Most of his friends also were bike heads, pot heads or artists. He had hired someone to do an amazing job on airbrushing a sexy lady on the gas tank. She looked sexy and blonde, just like Sue. Teddy was getting it worthy of entering in the Cleveland Auto Show the following January.

High school graduation came quickly. Lydia was not as excited as most of her friends who were going off to out-of-state colleges. She knew things would stay status quo for her in Cleveland. She still wanted to skate, stay close to her job at the print shop and stay close to Matt. She had enough changes when her parents decided to move out of their Cleveland Heights home and go 12 miles farther east. They wanted a yard, a garden, and the whole white picket fence dream. The new house belonged to a cousin on Marilyn's side and they got a deal they thought they could afford. Lydia didn't want to be out in what she called "boo-foo-Egypt" even though the house was a fairly straight shot east of the Hampshire house. It had an in-ground pool, large garden and a pond in the back. Still, this was not enticing enough for her to spend more than a couple of nights a week there. She always packed changes of clothes and running shoes to live out of the car her father had basically given her. With that Dodge, she could spend time with her brother at the print shop and Matt at the bar. Her sister, Christy, and her new family had taken over the house on Hampshire. Lydia often stayed in the Heights in the attic that used to be Teddy and Randy's room growing up. It was a way for Lydia to have the best of both worlds.

All the changes Teddy had made to his Triumph 750 were complete by fall of 1980. He entered the 1981 Cleveland Auto Show commonly known as The Autorama in January of '81. All of the family except Christy attended that year. She was busy that afternoon taking care of her responsibilities as a young mother of two. At the show, Noel fell in love with the Alpha Romeo and Fiat two-door cars. Marilyn and Randy looked completely bored and Lydia wanted each and every muscle car that she saw. She imagined herself behind the wheel of a Camaro, a Firebird or an old-style GTO. She took her father's Nikon and snapped as many pictures as she could on what was left of her father's role of film. Gone were the days of her cheap little Instamatic. She was a real photographer now and had even submitted some great candid shots of her friends in the courtyard for her high school yearbook.

Teddy won best of the show in the motorcycle chopper division with his loaded custom leather seat and that fantastic paint job. The engine was shinier than Noel's bald head and it was a marvel to be sure. The family celebrated with a dinner downtown. Marilyn pulled out her Entertainment Coupon Book that was as thick as a telephone book. She loved the two for one coupons and stuffed that book in the glove box of the family car for just such occasions. Teddy stored the bike during the snowy Cleveland winter and did not touch it until the following spring.

Winter turned into spring and spring into summer in the blink of an eye. In the fall Lydia had an opportunity to help teach Learn To Skate classes at the rink when another instructor was let go suddenly. She and Matt still seemed to have a secure relationship and her journey into adult life appeared seamless.

On a rather warm Friday evening in October, Matt and Liddy were on a date. As Matt pulled into the gas station near her home to fill up his car, she saw Teddy on the bike, with Sue on the back. There were no helmets on their heads or on the bike. They too were filling up their ride.

I should say something. Why don't they have their helmets on? I don't even see them on the sissy bar. I really should say something. No. Teddy won't want his little sister telling him what to do. Like he's gonna listen to me!

"Hey, Teddy!" Lydia said as she waved.

"Hey, kiddo. Hi, Matt," he responded.

"Where you goin'?"

"Over to Sue's house."

"And you?"

"Matt's taking me to a party."

"Be safe!" he reminded her.

"Always!" Matt said.

Those were the last words spoken to Teddy. The next morning there was a phone call to her parents from Teddy's friend Scott.

CHAPTER NINE

Cottage Grove

Noel walked over to the wall phone in the gold wallpapered dining room. On the other end of the receiver was a hysterical Scott saying that there had been an accident. Teddy and Scott had been riding their choppers in a strange little pocket of the Heights where there were stop signs every two or three houses. The street addresses went east-west but the street they were on, Cottage Grove, ran north-south so that the large houses were basically corner houses to the other streets. Lydia found out months later that they had been partying the night before that morning they left to go to a friend's house to watch a football game on TV.

Scott's bike was in front of Teddy's as they started, stopped, started and stopped again, every two or three houses. Teddy's front tire must have hit Scott's back tire and down Teddy went. With no helmet, his head had hit the curb hard. At the next stop sign, Scott no longer heard the roar of Teddy's bike, so he looked over his shoulder. Seeing Teddy down, he rushed back attending to him as best he could. He gave him mouth-to-mouth resuscitation. No one had cell phones at the time. A neighbor called the paramedics and the drive to the nearby hospital was fairly quick

Still, the news was bad. He was revived but had not yet registered a brainwave. The next few days would be critical. Telling Lydia was difficult. She was the baby of the family and worshiped the ground Teddy walked on. She begged to see him at the hospital. Initially, the answer was a big "no" from her parents because he was in the Intensive Care Unit. The following day she was allowed to go. Lydia prayed a lot since the phone call. It seemed inconceivable to her that he would not pull through. Her parents had neglected to tell her about the lack of brain activity, still hoping that there would be some sign of hope.

As Liddy, her sister Christy and her parents walked the long, sterile hall to Teddy's room, she mumbled one more prayer. Nothing had prepared her for what she stepped into. The blinds were drawn in the room, keeping the light muted. He was hooked up to several machines and his very swollen head was wrapped in bandages like a Frankenstein mummy. The bandage barely allowed an eye to peek through. The one eye she did see was shut and the lid purple from bruising. He seemed to be shaking as if he were very cold. She touched his hand. It did, indeed feel like he was freezing.

Why is he so cold? Why don't they put more blankets on him?

Almost as if on cue, the nurse arrived and told her parents that they were keeping him cold to reduce the brain swelling. Marilyn began to cry and Noel began to pray silently. Lydia and Christy were in disbelief. His body was fine. He had a minor injury to his right leg, but all systems seemed normal otherwise. Her father told her to talk to Teddy in case he could hear while in the coma. Marilyn began talking through the tears and Noel joined in, but Lydia just refused to accept that any of this was really happening.

The next couple of days were agonizing for the whole family. In the end, if there was no registered brainwave by day three, then Marilyn and Noel had to decide if they would keep him on life support or let him go to God. The decision was made to let him go, and so very many details were kept from poor Lydia. Everyone wanted to spare her the grief they were all experiencing, still thinking of her as a little girl and not like the high school graduate and college student that she saw herself as.

The news of his passing hit Lydia like a wrecking ball smashing through a plywood house. Stages of grief were taking turns on her, but especially anger. First, she blamed herself for not telling him to wear his helmet the night before she and Matt had seen him at the gas station. Next, she blamed God. She cursed Him out loud with venom in her voice and fists flailing about. She could not fathom that the loving God her father always talked about would take her favorite grandparent and now her favorite sibling.

The hell with this! Why? Why? WHY? It was Teddy! I can't live without him. He always stuck up for me when Randy was being an ass. He had everything going for him. Look at mom now. She is a wreck. Everyone says kids are never supposed to die first. What the hell, God?

That Sunday she went through the motions of going to church with her family but she did not sing. She watched from the sidelines as her parents planned the funeral in Pennsylvania where he would be buried near Grandpa Abe. The memorial would be at their church in Cleveland, fully understanding that most of their friends and family would not make a four-hour drive for the burial.

Scott, Teddy's girlfriend Sue and a couple other close friends of Teddy's drove in a caravan for the burial. The drive would have been beautiful if it were for any other reason. The leaves on the trees were all turning colors and the winds made the blades dance and sway before hitting the cold ground. The hills of Pennsylvania were gorgeous and sad at the same time giving off their pigment to leave nothing other than hues of ugly brown for a long, long winter.

Pulling up to Grandpa Abe's headstone gave Lydia a chill that felt more like December than October. It truly sickened her to see that her grandmother's name was already on the tombstone next to Abe's with only her birthdate. The stone was just waiting for her to die to complete its destiny as a marker of death.

Liddy stood by Randy this time as the pastor read the typical verses she would hear all too often in her life. Trying to stay stoic, Liddy looked to her right and saw that Sue was in hysterics. No one knew how to calm her down so they just let her wail uncontrollably. For a brief moment, it looked like she would jump on his casket and go right down with him. Family members began placing single roses on the casket. Scott walked over to the grave and kissed a lucky rabbit's foot and placed it on the casket. Lydia buried her head in Randy's jacket when she saw that it was time for the casket to be lowered. Too many similarities from when she was 11. She allowed the tears to flow as the reality of "ashes to ashes and dust to dust" made it to the forefront of her brain. This was real. This was forever. How could she go on with her other brother she had so little in common with and a sister 12 years older, so busy with her own growing family?

The next two days she slept quite a bit and wrote in her diary. She was no poet. Still, she penned a free verse in her diary that read:

> *Teddy*
> *Stupid metal box.*
> *There lies my sweet bother.*
> *All messed up forever.*

The following week was the memorial service at the church that Noel and all of his children had been baptized in. The service was planned in the small chapel off to the right side of the main sanctuary, but it was soon apparent by the crowd that they would have to move it to the main sanctuary. Marilyn was relieved that she had printed 200 memorial service programs at the print shop, and yet they still ran out. Almost the entire lower level of the Epworth Euclid United Methodist Church seemed filled with family, print shop customers, leather jacket wearing bikers, and people from the community that were also in astonishment that such a young life was taken.

Aaron and Roger came and sat together, but Lydia stayed with her family and only shot them glances of approval as if to say thank you for coming. Matt sat with the family, as he had begun to get to know Lydia's parents and the relationship was no longer a secret. Naturally, Sue also sat with the family in the front row and in the receiving line.

Later, she wrote:

Dear Diary,

We were all amazed at how many people came, both young and old. Lots of printing customers, church people, school friends and extended family. I never want to ever go through a young death again and yet I never want to forget the way I felt today. I felt as if Teddy were floating right above me listening and watching it all. The preacher tried to make it light and all by saying "If God needed anything in Heaven fixed, Teddy would be there to fix it like he did with cars and printing presses." I held Randy's hand. He cried a lot. I didn't. At home, some people came over and ate food and told little stories about Teddy.

Weeks went by and Lydia seemed okay. On the nights that she stayed in the new home, she and her father still ran together the following morning. Noel noticed that she no longer chattered away during the runs and had lost a bit of weight. He worried about her. A parent's love can be an amazing and astute thing. When he sensed that the time was right, he sat Liddy down at the kitchen table and began to explain his concern for her well being. He asked her if she could help him find something positive that came out of Teddy's death.

What? Is he out of his flippin' mind? We are talking about Teddy. You know, 26-year-old, cute, funny, sweet, Teddy!

"Daddy! What?"

"Well, I was thinking that finding something positive that came from Teddy's death could help us move through this better," Noel said.

I don't want to move through this. I just want Teddy back. I just want to wake up from this horrible dream.

"I don't get it." She replied.

The pregnant pause was palpable as her father simply allowed her 17-year-old brain to process the request.

"It's not fair!" she blurted out. "He was going to marry Sue!"

"Yes, but I suppose it is a good thing that he did not leave behind a wife and children to have no husband and father."

Lydia was quick to dismiss this and said: "He just started those video and filmmaking classes at college and was going to make something of himself."

"Oh, we all know that school or no school, Teddy had many gifts, that's for sure. He didn't need a piece of paper on a wall for us to know that he was smart."

"He was just starting to go to church with us again," Lydia pouted.

"Ah, yes, and what a blessing that he was getting right with God before he was taken from this earthly life," was Noel's calm reply.

"He even quit smoking! He was young! He was running with us. He was healthy!" Lydia tried to lob back answers like a ball at a tennis match, but Noel was an expert at spiritual tennis. His response was of tenderness and love as he said: "Were you aware that Teddy was an organ donor? Because he was young and healthy the loss of his life has saved several people or given them better lives. The doctor said that his donation can help with eyes, kidneys, liver, heart and even skin. Thank goodness that he was young and healthy."

It was pointless to argue with her father. She knew in her heart of hearts that he was right. She tried to get up from the table but Noel gently placed his hand on her arm and looked her straight in the eyes. Lydia sat back down but lowered her head. She did not want to face this reality. "Lydia, there is something that I think every Christian needs to know. People always ask 'Why did God take my son or daughter or mother or father?' When in reality a loving God would not do these things. I can tell you that the God I know does not start wars, create disease, cause divorce or take young lives. Instead, he gives us free will and out of our lifestyle choices come the difficult times. It is how we choose to react to adversity that allows for healing."

Later that evening out came the diary.

> *Dad, if you are reading this, STOP! It's my diary. I know what you said sounds logical, but I still don't get things like how a baby could get cancer or like how a hurricane could wipe out a whole town. That's just not a lifestyle choice. I still think it stinks that he's gone and I sort of feel like he is still just above me, watching or something. But I'll try to get through this somehow.*

Sue brought several large boxes over to the print shop one afternoon in November. Her eyes were bloodshot from crying. They were filled with Teddy's things. Lydia went through them with her father and begged for several items. As morbid as it was to look through her dead brother's life condensed into nothing but cardboard boxes she wanted anything that even remotely fit her. She took most of his Levi's jeans knowing they would be too big. She kept several of his T-shirts, his leather jacket and a sterling silver ring with turquoise and alabaster triangles around it. The ring was also too big, but she would never part with it. The clothing still smelled of British Sterling and the coconut hand lotion he was so fond of. She wore those items again and again over the next several months until she could no longer smell him.

Late that same November, Matt and two of his friends rented a house in the city next to Cleveland Heights. Lydia often spent as long as she could there until the last moment before her curfew at her old home where she often stayed with her sister, Christy and her husband or her curfew at the new house. Her mother and Christy had worked out an agreement for Lydia that no matter where she was spending the night, there would be a curfew.

As the sun was setting, Matt and Lydia sat out on the small back porch of Matt's rental house and cuddled under a thick blanket. He began to tell her a story he could barely believe himself.

"Liddy, you won't believe this, but you know my cousin John? Well, my other cousin, his sister, Kathy, saw a spiritualist last week. This weird spiritual lady said that she was getting a message that a brother of a friend of a family member who had died in a motorcycle accident wanted to tell his family that he is doing okay and that they can stop worrying about him."

Lydia got the chills as he continued his story. So my cousin Kathy had no idea what the hell she was talking about but she told John anyway. John knows your brother Randy. So John told me and now I am telling you!"

"I am speechless!"

The two held hands under the blanket as Liddy began to cry. Matt pulled her hand out from under the blanket and put it up to his eyes. He wanted to show her that he was crying too. She knew it was getting late and called her parents to ask if she could stay in her old home instead of making the drive to the new one. She told her parents about the spiritualist but she wanted to tell Christy in person.

That very same evening, Noel had parked his car in the horseshoe driveway of the new home. He, Marilyn and Randy retired to their rooms early. Later in the evening, there was a strange clicking sound outside, coming from the driveway. Randy up in his room thought it was his parents, and his parents in their room though it was Randy tossing and turning in his bed. When the rhythmic clicking continued, the three curious sleepyheads met in the hallway and crept downstairs. Opening the big, brown front door, they stepped outside and stared at their Oldsmobile incredulously. The locks of the grey beast were clicking up and down, up and down, over and over. Noel reached to open the door and it locked on him. He stared in disbelief, but remembering the story Lydia had told him earlier, he just began talking to the car.

"Teddy, if this is you, we understand. Teddy, we love you. Teddy, we will always miss you but we heard you are fine and you can go now." With his hand still on the door of the Regency, the clicking stopped and Noel was able to open the door. Marilyn was in tears. Randy led her back into the house and Noel began brewing coffee.

"Oh, Noel, it's too late for coffee," Marilyn said.

"Honey, I have a feeling none of us will be sleeping tonight."

Around the small kitchen table, the three sat and talked about how all Teddy ever loved was working on cars. Logic told them that their car may have had an electrical short. But their imaginative minds told them that it was Teddy asking if it was okay to go on.

There were other times where his presence was felt rather profoundly, but none more than the dreams Lydia would have over the next couple of years. The brightness and clarity of the dreams dimmed over time, but Teddy visited for years through Lydia's dreams. He would come briefly to catch up with her and then ascend back to where he came from.

Dear Teddy,

Where do I begin? You were the brother who never judged or teased. I know I must have driven you crazy following you around and doing everything within my power to emulate you. We were nine years apart and that could not have been fun during your teenage years when a little girl would pop out from behind the couch when you were trying to make out with your girlfriend, or when you just wanted to be with Sue and I insisted on tagging along to some movie or concert.

I will never forget how protective you were of me and how when Randy and I would fight, you always took my side. Poor Randy. I can remember a couple of smackdowns that he most likely did not deserve.

As I write this being a fully grown woman, I wanted to thank you for allowing me to just be that grubby, little tomboy who had no idea what she would become. I never had to fake it around you, never had to act a certain way and never had to be anything but your little sis. I loved that role and regret that I only got to play it for 17 years.

I still see you at the age of 26 although now you would be in your 60s. I still look up to you and hope that you are smiling down on me and proud of the decisions I am making as a mom, wife and occasional tomboy!

I miss you after all of these years and most likely always will. I gave my only son your name as his middle name to honor you and to remember that Theodore means God-given or God's gift. I hope that my Nicholas Theodore grows up to be the deep thinker, smart and loving person that you were.

Love, Lydia

CHAPTER TEN
Beginnings and Endings

Lydia's relationship with Matt grew and grew until she thought she would burst. She and Noel were running one morning and Lydia wanted some sort of approval from her dad to take her relationship to the next level with Matt. She worked into the conversation some carefully planned questions about his own relationship with Marilyn when they were dating.

Noel was no dummy and knew just what to say to keep her hormones at bay. Often, when she tried to ask questions about him, they were really about her. He said, "Well, I know this will sound very old-fashioned and corny. I'm okay with that. But you see daughter, I was in love with being in love. I used to fall so hard for each and every girl I met. I used to think 'This is the one,' then we would break up and I would think the next one was 'the one.'" He continued, "One time I was so ga-ga for a girl in my class that I asked my mom to forbid me to see her."

"What?" Lydia asked.

"Well, that way I knew I had an excuse not to go too far. I told her at school the next day that I was sorry we had to break up, but my mother forbade me to date."

"Oh, brother," Liddy said as she rolled her eyes and picked up the pace a little bit. She did not like where this conversation was headed.

"The other thing was this. You see I always wanted to marry a virgin. I decided that in order for that to be fair, I should present myself as a virgin too. Believe me, I had plenty of chances to, um, well, you know. When I was in Guam during World War Two, there were always women who wanted to be intimate with us sailors, but I refrained."

Liddy was really regretting bringing this up, but Noel was on point when he said, "You know what the best part is?"

"No."

"Because your mother and I were virgins when we married, we have never been with anyone else. I have nothing to compare her to. She has nothing to compare me to. She has been the best lover in the world to me because of that."

"I guess that's a really good point, dad." And she let it go at that.

The rest of the run was spent trying to talk about anything but Matt and sex. As awkward as the conversation was, she knew she never had conversations like that with her mom. Marilyn could not even talk to her about puberty when it hit. She had Liddy ask her sister, Christy, who was much easier to talk to anyway.

Lydia's training now began to include swimming and biking. She had seen some crazy event on television where insane people would swim in the Pacific ocean for 2.4 miles, hop on a bike and ride through the hot lava highways of the big island of Kona, Hawaii for 112 miles and then run a full 26.2 mile marathon. She hoped to be able to do that event someday and began training in earnest. Liddy was finishing more college classes, working two part-time jobs and truly becoming an independent woman.

On a sunny morning in the spring, she popped over to Matt's house. He was washing his car like he always did before a date with her. Funny thing was, they did not have plans. Matt knew she had to work later at the local mall and she had just popped over unannounced. She went in to get a drink when the phone rang.

"Hello?"

"Hi, this is Tammy at Bridlewood Stables. I am just confirming your reservation for two today to horseback ride."

"Um, hang on," Lydia said as she put down the receiver.

"Matt, who are you horseback riding with?" Lydia bellowed out the window.

"Matt raced in and grabbed the phone from the table, mumbled to the woman and hung up.

"Oh, just someone from work," he said sheepishly.

"Boy or girl," she prompted. No answer.

"Boy or girl?" she demanded.

"It's just some girl that I got fixed up with," he said, quite defensively.

It was revealed at that moment when Matt tried to explain how his work friend had "fixed him up" that Matt either had no backbone or no longer loved her. His work friend story just seemed implausible. He was grasping at straws lying about how he had told this friend that he was already in a serious relationship.

The subsequent break up did nothing for Lydia's self-esteem. Here she had been working so hard on finding her place in her femininity, and this man that she adored was telling her that he needed a woman who really needed him.

"But, I *do* need you, Matt," she cried.

"No, you *want* me. There is a difference. This girl *needs* me."

"I don't get it. Explain!"

He continued to put into words how this new woman was basically a doormat who needed some man to rely on. He said that Lydia was too independent and strong for him. He didn't feel needed. That hurt. David from ninth grade was too weak for her, Aaron from high school was too gay for her, and now Matt was too insecure for her. Yet all she wanted was a good man in her life and for the opportunity to be able to hop on a motorcycle one day and be a demure and flirty Godess the next day. Why wouldn't anyone love her just the way she was?

Weeks went by when Lydia did nothing but scheme and plot at how to win Matt back. Who did she have to become? What did she have to act like to win him back? She called him and then popped over saying something lame like she had left an album at his house. Sometimes she would ask if she could borrow something. It was just pitiful. The most desperate attempt was one night when she decided to frequent the same bar that the two of them used to go to regularly. She did not dress up. She wanted to run into him and show him what a mess she had become without his love. Tragically, perhaps she thought she could guilt him back into her life.

She rode her skateboard up the hill from her parents' print shop to the bar known as "the place to be on Lee," The Colony. Matt had moved on. He was with his new woman on her side of town, miles and miles away both figuratively and literally. Frustrated, Lydia decided to just finish her beer and play the Laser Cue pinball game that she had gotten quite proficient at. Some dude was hogging the machine. When she finally slapped a quarter down and asked the player if she could play the next game, he turned to her and her heart began to race harder and faster. She felt her cheeks get warm and suddenly wished she had not dressed like what her brother, Randy, called a "bull-dyke."

There stood an Adonis with dark, wavy hair, at least 6 inches taller than she was, and wearing a short-sleeved shirt that made his biceps bulge. A flat stomach (no beer belly like Matt had) and a priceless grin sent her skyrocketing to the moon.

Still keeping a diary, it read: *I met the most amazing man tonight. His name is Vince. I have no idea how to get together with him again, but as God as my witness, I will be playing pinball every day until I see him in there again! We talked for a while and played a few games together. I won most of them.*

Duh! I'm on that game like white on rice. Anyway, I pray he goes there again soon.

"I just want a small wedding. Nothing fancy. I'll wear a dress but I'm not gonna wear the dumb veil. And the dress has to be the regular length. No flowy crap," Lydia announced to Randy one year and nine months after the pinball encounter with Vince.

Since Teddy's death, she had become much closer to Randy. She missed Teddy miserably, but Randy had grown up and was no longer the obnoxious big brother who poked her on car rides and used fancy language to make her feel stupid. She had come to terms with his being gay, although she still did not want to hear about his escapades. She had already heard enough from Aaron who constantly overshared and had too many partners to count.

Randy took an off-white, tea-length dress he had given Lydia for one of her birthdays, and asked for it back. He knew just what to do with the lace sleeves and bodice.

"I'll bead the lace sleeves and dress up the front. Are you sure you don't want a veil? You would look so amazing," he told her.

"No, I hate the symbolism of the damned thing. It's archaic and it's only gonna be immediate family, so what's the point?" she retorted.

Even after all of these years, she still grappled with wanting to look amazing, feminine, girly and wonderful. She wanted to turn to her new husband and be everything he would ever want, yet she could not bear the thought of people actually seeing her in a dress. She still had no idea how to put makeup on properly, and why would she?

You're just gonna sweat it off when you go running or swimming.

The wedding took place between two trees in the backyard of Marlyn and Noel's home. It was indeed just the immediate family of Lydia along with Vince's parents. Liddy's longtime figure skating friend, Heather, stood as the Maid of Honor and Randy stood as the Best Man when Vince's brother could not find the address in time for the ceremony. Still in wedding attire, that evening Vince and Lydia went to Vince's 10-year high school reunion. What a wonderful time they had telling everyone that had just wed hours earlier.

The following day they held the reception in her parent's backyard. Liddy's parents rented a tent and arranged finger foods and cake for about 50 friends and extended family. The weather was wonderful and as soon as everyone had seen Liddy in her dress, she took it right off and donned a swimsuit to jump into the family pool. Noel made a joke about taking the bridal plunge. Liddy swam with the younger cousins and played badminton in the front yard with some of their mutual friends. Nothing fancy. Just fun and games. Just the way she and Vince liked it. She had fallen for a man that loved nothing more than to run, bike, kayak, rock climb and shoot a bow and arrow. It was heaven on earth that she found someone even more active than she was.

Aaron was not able to attend the wedding reception but had sent a lovely glass bowl from The May Company. Lydia was so excited to be married but felt a slight sadness as she knew her silly days of hanging out with the guys was long over. She remained friends with Aaron from a distance but they had grown farther and farther apart as he became entrenched in his lifestyle choices and Lydia with her new husband. One day out of the blue, Roger called Lydia to say that Aaron had been sick for a while and had died. Dare she say it? Was it AIDS? Yes, the 1980s was rampant with what people were calling "gay man's cancer." Aaron died a single man and had barely reached his mid-20s.

Vince had only met Aaron once or twice as the friendship between Aaron and Liddy had been waning, so Liddy did not even think to invite her husband to the funeral home. Liddy arrived on time but there was very limited seating, so she sat next to strangers. Other than it being Jewish, the similarities between Teddy's funeral and Aaron's was uncanny. Packed in like sardines.

Beginnings and Endings

People crying. Running out of programs. It was a lovely service and all of the prayers in Hebrew brought back fond memories of her Jewish Montessori School experience.

Instead of taking the direct route home, Lydia drove around their old haunts and just thought about the good and the bad times. Most of the time he was so much fun, but there were some frustrating times too when he was cruel to her or teased her clothing choices and called her a lesbian. He often flirted with her brother Randy, right in front of her. Even though they had made out a few times, he didn't seem interested in her as a girlfriend, yet he got intensely jealous when she would have a boyfriend or kiss another boy. It was a strange relationship to be sure, but it was glorious in its own weird way and he would be missed. Their bond transcended understanding. She lamented his death, and let the tears roll gently down her cheeks, spilling onto her dress pants.

What would I do without you, my journal? These last couple of years have symbolized a beginning and an end. It has been the beginning of my marriage and now the end of Aaron's life. It has been the end of an era of hanging around my male friends. Vince is super trusting that any man I hang out with is just a friend, but as I get closer to understanding what a real marriage is about, I have no desire to hang out with any other males besides my own husband and my brother, Randy. It's so sad how I had not kept in touch with Roger and had no idea that Aaron was even sick. I wish I remembered what our last conversation was about. Well, I guess that overused saying is accurate. Hindsight is 20/20.

Dear Aaron,

That was a wild ride, high school, huh? You and I. Joni Mitchell. Carly Simon. The B-52's. Sitting on the swings in the playground by your home. Streaking at the country club. Hanging out with Roger. Throwing each other into Roger's pool. Watching

Saturday Night Live *at our own homes but talking on the phone the whole time. Do you remember our 64-day record of never missing a phone call to each other? I was furious when we fought and broke that record.*

I remember the progression of you telling me that you were straight, then you said "I swing both ways," but Randy and I knew you were just trying to find yourself and that more than likely you were not swinging my way. Eventually, when you let us all know you were gay, I was already enamored with you and figured at least I got a great friend out of the deal.

I could not stand my brother Randy as a child because I had no idea what to feel about him being so different. But, falling for you made me less of a judgemental bitch. Perhaps you helped me to accept Randy more. You were so funny, animated, smart, cunning, and yes, sometimes outright mean. But Aaron, I want to thank you for being in my life. Thank you for showing me that your feelings were as valid as mine. Your pain was as real as mine. Your crushes were as hard as mine and your love was as strong as mine. The things you told me and the secrets you trusted me with were precious to me. I will never forget you.

Love, Lydia

CHAPTER ELEVEN
No More Free Copies

As the late '80s and early '90s approached, life at the print shop took a turn for the worst. National chain stores like Kinko's (now FedEx Office) were popping up everywhere. They were out pricing mom and pop print shops with their Xerox copy services, FAX machines and quick delivery. Home computers were also becoming increasingly more sophisticated with programs that let people do much of their basic printing for a fraction of the cost. The only things that kept the business afloat were the loyalty of their favorite customers and the need for fancy wedding invitations, that were still generally ordered from catalogs and farmed out for a marked-up price or printed in-house. Vince became a printer and learned from the best, Lydia and Noel.

Lydia still taught ice skating lessons part-time but was busy with the two children they had at the time. Randy was incredible with the girls, Kristen and Kaitlyn. When Lydia had to teach skating lessons, Kristen had a little desk and toy box she busied herself with set up at the shop. Baby Kaitlyn had a portable playpen set up in the back of the shop where Vince could check on his princesses in between press runs. Randy was the best at rocking Kaitlyn to sleep when he wasn't stripping negatives at his light table. Naturally, Grandma Marilyn and Grandpa Noel were also willing to play with and love their grandchildren when not attending to customers in the front office.

Randy had noticed a strange white spot at the base of his nose. An appointment with the dermatologist revealed a small skin cancer. Quick to remove it, Randy had plastic surgery where the growth was removed and biopsied, while a small piece of facial muscle was stretched upward to prevent a disfiguring scar. The doctors seemed baffled. With cancer, there is usually a primary site and a secondary site or primary cancer and secondary cancer. They suspected that the skin cancer was secondary cancer yet they were not sure where the primary cancer was lurking.

Shortly after Randy's facial surgery, the print shop closed. No more free copies, birthday invitations or free babysitting. Vince and Randy had to find work elsewhere and Lydia now had to drag her children to the rink with her instead of relying on her built-in babysitters. To add to all of the changes that were happening, she found out that she was pregnant. Baby Nick would round out the Thorpe family. By the time Nicholas was born, Randy had begun to show some other disturbing signs besides a facial scar. When he turned his head to the left, the lymph nodes on the right side of his neck bulged a bit. When he turned his head to the right, the nodes on the left side of his neck bulged a bit.

Back to the doctor he went. There were biopsies and tests. Lydia was spared much of the information perhaps once more because they wanted to spare the baby of the family any grief, or perhaps because Marilyn, Noel and Randy figured that she was so busy with her own young family. Marilyn was also dealing with her own diagnosis of Parkinson's Disease and Noel was becoming increasingly forgetful.

No More Free Copies

Christy and her family had moved to Miami a few years earlier, so she missed the closing of the shop. She and her husband had a third child there. Vince and Lydia had purchased a small home in the Heights and invited Randy and the parents over for each and every milestone their children achieved. Randy was the quintessential perfect uncle. He never missed a birthday, ballet recital or award given to those sweet Thorpe children. He spoiled them rotten and had a special bond with all three. He never played favorites and spent money he barely had on treats, gifts and books for them.

Randy had a life partner who the children referred to as Uncle Rick. The parents treated him as another son and life seemed as perfect as it could be until the next round of tests came back. More cancer and with lymphatic involvement. There would be surgery, but Randy had no interest in chemotherapy. He was an excellent candidate for an experimental treatment, so he signed up for that.

One Sunday Lydia asked a woman at her church to pray for her brother. The woman asked about his symptoms and signs, as well as previous treatments. Liddy assumed it was because she wanted all of the details to pray more fervently. Imagine her surprise when the friend said, "Lydia, I think your brother may have AIDS."

"No, it's skin cancer. Melanoma," she said. All the while Liddy was seething inside that her friend might be right and that once again she was left out of adult family conversations.

She had to drive Randy from her parents home back into the Heights later that afternoon, so she bluntly asked if he was HIV positive. Yes. Did he have AIDS? Yes. Was the skin cancer just a ruse? No.

"Liddy, I'm a mess. I do have melanoma and part of the reason that the experimental drugs may not be working that well is that my immune system is weak from the HIV status. I didn't mean to keep this from you."

"Oh, like hell! This is the same shit as when Mom got her Parkinson's diagnosis. No one told me until she teetered and tottered into a wall one day and I yelled at her for being so out of shape that she didn't have good balance. Dad jumped all over me telling me that I did not know the whole story. You know why? Because no one told me the whole story! I am not a baby anymore. I am a grown-ass woman. Why does everyone think I can't handle the truth?" she screamed.

"I don't know sis,"

"It's embarrassing to find out about you from someone who has never even met you. I looked so ignorant as I was defending you. Haven't you been with Rick for years?"

"Yes, but I have not always been faithful to him. I was with so many people before we even met and now there is all of this information about how HIV can be dormant for so many years before anyone has any symptoms. Believe me, I tried to like girls all my life. I dated them and took them to prom but I always felt like I was born in the wrong body or even the wrong time period or something. They didn't need me to open the car door for them or pay for their dinner. I felt displaced like I didn't know what my role as a male was. And then one night, my friend Craig and I snuck into his parent's liquor cabinet. We got a little drunk and started wrestling. Things started happening and I felt such relief that we felt so right together. Even so, I would not wish this lifestyle on anyone. It's hard. The teasing, the gay bashing, the secrets, and the fact that I will never have kids like you and Vince. It's all very difficult," he confided.

Lydia just drove without comment. The whole world had changed for her at that moment as she realized that she may lose brother number two. This would be a huge test of her faith in God, as she knew it would not only be hard for her, but hard for her mother if she were to outlive both of her sons.

Changing the subject, she asked, "So what's going on with Dad? Does he have some disease that you guys are hiding from me too? He seems really out of it sometimes and Mom has been calling me out to their house sometimes to do the stuff dad used to do all the time, like mow the lawn or put the pool chemicals in the pool."

"Well, I'll tell you all that I know. He did have a little fender bender at the bottom of Wilson Mills and River Road last month and he got lost on his four-mile run once. He seems fairly normal during the day, but he hangs on Mom and follows her everywhere in the evening," he answered.

"Has he been to the doctor?"

"No, but I made Mom promise that if he did anything weirder than his normal weirdness, that she had better take him to the Cleveland Clinic."

Noel's test at the Cleveland Clinic was arduous. Marilyn and Lydia were not allowed to be in the room with him so they drove around downtown and found a nice place to have lunch with the kids while he had cognitive testing done. He was still in the test center when they returned, but results were only preliminary. Marilyn was quite curious to know what they did so when Noel was in the car for the drive home, he tried to explain things about the test as best as he could remember them. It was funny and sad all at once as they realized that he was far worse than they thought.

"They had these cards and they only had heads!" he exclaimed and then continued,

"There were no bodies on them. I had to say who they were and I just knew they needed their bodies."

He continued to talk about a clock he had to draw, something he had to do with numbers and those darned cards with the heads. He went on and on about how they had no bodies.

Lydia called Randy and said that the test administrator said that he most likely had a lot of people fooled for a long time simply because he was convivial and warm. They were concerned that he did, in fact, have dementia, not ruling out Alzheimer's.

Over the course of the next year, family meetings did not include Noel. Lydia was tired of driving 12 miles to dump chemicals in a pool, go back home only to hear the answering machine say that she needed to go back out there to take the garbage from the garage to the curb for Thursday morning garbage pick up.

"Mom, are you kidding?" she called back. "Have dad do it. I was just out there."

"Honey, I have tried explaining it to him several times. He just doesn't know what I am asking him to do. I even tried to do it myself but with my Parkinson's, I just don't have the strength," she said, exasperated.

At the next meeting, Randy suggested that the Thorpes move out of the Heights and in with the parents. Vince was not keen on living with his in-laws. Lydia was not keen on leaving the Heights where all of her best memories were and where she brought each of her babies home from the hospital to their house on Northampton Road.

"Well, I think it is no big secret that I will never be married or have kids. Rick and I don't need that big of a property. I know I am no longer strong enough to help much with the big stuff like mowing and tree trimming. You have the kids and they would love the pond and pool and garden. It's a safe place for them to grow up and the school system is great out there," Randy argued.

Marilyn spoke up: "We can move our bedroom downstairs where the office is and we would have our own bathroom. You guys would share the kitchen and laundry room, but we could also put up a dividing wall where the sunroom is. Dad and I could have the sunroom as our living room and you guys can have the formal living room when your family needs privacy. The girls can share a room, Nick can have a room and you and Vince can take the upstairs master bedroom."

It seemed to Lydia like Randy and Marilyn had already done everything shy of calling the contractor out to put up the dividing wall. It would take prayerful consideration and more discussion as well as getting their Cleveland Heights home ready for sale.

CHAPTER TWELVE

Powerless

It seemed as if the hands of God wanted this move more than Lydia and Vince. Their house sold before they even had an open house, and friends were more than happy to purchase a fair chunk of their furniture and baby toys that Nick, now 2, had no use for.

Watching Randy's melanoma and AIDS and Noel's dementia deteriorate at the same time was just too difficult for Lydia. She felt so powerless about her brother and father. Liddy's escape was her three children, so she busied herself with putting them into every activity they had a propensity for. She had decided that even though they had moved into a great school system, she wanted to homeschool them at least for a few years. She and Vince also spent a good bit of time in the maintenance of the one-acre property that they had now acquired from her parents. Lydia had to take Noel and Marilyn to many doctor appointments as the aging process was not kind to either of them.

Christy, now divorced, was living in California and had begun a whole new career in the holistic healing arts. Lydia thought that Christy was ideally suited for this, as she had always been the freewheeling child of the '60s and quite the nonconformist. Marilyn had called Christy to see if she could afford a visit as Randy was doing so poorly.

Christy was in the middle of a class when her mother called, so she promised to book a flight the next day. Her class was with the International Order of St. Luke the Physician, of which Christy was a member. The class was studying all the healing miracles of Jesus. That night the class was supposed to be on the long-distance healing of Jesus, but someone asked a question about exorcising demons. Most modern people believe that "demons" is a euphemism for mental illness. So the teacher said that the exorcism study group was scheduled for a later date, but since the student had brought up the subject, he decided to do that class then and there. It was amazing, as he explained that yes, sometimes it could be mental illness, but that didn't negate the existence of demons and true evil. He taught the class how to rebuke any possessing spirits. It must never be done alone and there must always be strong prayer warriors around. Christy was fascinated, but it never occurred to her that the Holy Spirit had arranged for her to have that lesson on that evening.

The next day she arrived in Cleveland and went straight to the Palliative Care Unit of Metro Hospital. Randy was in a stupor until he heard the sound of Christy moving the heavy chair closer to his bed.

"Is that you, Chris?" he said as he tried to sit up.

"Yes," she said choking back a tear.

Christy could not believe what she saw. From the waist up, Randy looked like an Auschwitz survivor. From the waist down, he was swollen like the Michelin man. The doctors had just had a consult, and two walked into the room and introduced themselves as they poked around with Randy and wrote some notes on the chart at the end of his bed. Christy asked if there were any contraindications to her doing some massage and aromatherapy. She felt a bit of a condescending tone as they said, "No, go ahead, do whatever." Christy was sure they thought he would be dead soon anyway. The nurse had just taken his blood count, and it was really off.

Christy pulled from her carry-on bag a blend of aromatherapy oils to help oxygenate his blood. An hour later the nurse came back, and Randy's reading had improved tremendously. The edema in his legs and groin was still profound so the next step was for Christy to do some lymphatic drainage on him. Soon after this gentle kind of massage, he was able to pee like a race horse and the swelling was greatly reduced.

"Christy!" he shouted from the bathroom, "I can see my penis!" She laughed as he must have been too swollen to have seen it before.

The next day Lydia's cousin Gail was already visiting in the room with Randy when she and Marilyn had arrived. He was sound asleep and Gail began to talk about the conversation they had shared before he dozed.

"We talked about God. We talked about his lifestyle choices and he confessed a lot of things he really regretted. I told him that all he had to do was to ask God for forgiveness. He was quite animated in telling me that he had already come to Jesus a while ago. He even told me that he knew that Jesus had forgiven him of his sins, but that he could not seem to forgive himself," Gail said.

"Oh, that's not good for him emotionally," Christy commented.

Hearing voices, Randy awoke and thankfully looked less like a Holocaust victim, and more like her dear brother. Randy started crying and saying that he felt he was possessed. The hairs on Christy's arms stood up with goosebumps. She gravely assured him that it was possible, per the lesson she had taken the night before. Was this part of the reason why he could not forgive himself?

"There are some energies or entities that seem attracted to certain places like a house, but others seem drawn to certain illnesses," Christy said. "And there are some that just move in when the host is too physically and spiritually drained to resist.

So Randy, do you want me to see if we can release some of those energies?" she asked. He readily agreed.

Christy had Mom and Gail hold his hands and pray. She started sweeping her hands down his body starting from Randy's head to his toes and demanding in the name of Jesus Christ that whatever entities were present in Randy had to leave, return to God, and bother no one else along the way. She continued doing that for several minutes, building up the intensity as her faith flowed freely. Initially, Randy shuddered and shook like he was cold. He exclaimed that he saw vibrant, unearthly, horrible colors as they were passing over him. His moaning and wailing startled his reserved cousin and mother.

When Christy finished, she allowed Randy to calm down and stop shaking. She asked him, "Tell me more about the colors you were talking about."

"Oh, Christy! I can't even describe them because I had never seen these colors. They were dark and horrible. They were putrid. They were like combinations of chartreuse and vomit, brown and rust, but worse. They floated over me. Finally, they started getting a bit lighter and I even saw a few pastels. But, Oh! Christy! I saw them! I swear I really saw them!"

"You saw what?"

"I saw the hands of God!"

"What?"

"Yes, I saw them. And do you know what? They looked just like Grandpa's hands."

You could hear a pin drop at that moment as no one in the room knew what to say.

When Christy told Lydia and Vince about her day at the hospital, Lydia felt an unspeakable joy amidst the pain of knowing the only brother she had left was not long for this world. She never forgot how hard-working her Grandpa's hands were with all of the calluses and cracks around the fingernails and found comfort in knowing that Randy saw God or Grandpa, or just maybe both.

Isn't that just like God to have rough, hard-working, hands like Grandpa? He works so hard for his children who all continually fail him in some way or another. Still, he never gives up on us. Lord, please, never give up on Randy!

Christy stayed a few more days but had to return to her practice or lose clients. Randy stayed about four more days in the Palliative Unit and then was discharged because he appeared to not be immediately terminal.

Close to one month later Christy returned for Father's Day, arriving Sunday afternoon, where she was met at the airport by Randy's partner, Rick. He warned her that it didn't look good. When Christy had left her brother a month prior, Randy had regained his look of health and well-being, but apparently, that was just a temporary reprieve. By this visit, Randy had home hospice set up and was basically on death watch in his two story apartment. His partner, Rick had moved a bed downstairs so that Randy did not have to attempt stairs anymore. The dining room table was moved into another room so that Randy could be by the door, the kitchen and a bathroom. Christy met the hospice nurse who quite frankly stated that Randy was in the "active dying" stage, which could mean he might pass later that day, the next day, or even up to a week later. She gave Christy a bottle of liquid morphine with a dropper, saying, "Give him a dropperful under his tongue every 3 hours, *or as needed.*" Christy interpreted this as meaning, rules didn't matter now, and hastening his death wouldn't be the worst outcome! He was too weak to travel to his parents home for Father's Day so Marilyn asked if they should move the celebration down to Randy's home. When Christy saw how bad Randy looked, she felt like sparing Marilyn the bleak outlook and told her not to come, that he was too weak for a party. Besides, there was no room for a crowd because of the hospital bed in the living room. She also worried about her father getting lost or being problematic. By that point in his dementia, he hardly knew who anyone was anymore.

"Is Lydia around?" Christy asked.

"Sure. Lydia!" Marilyn called.

"Hello?"

"Hey, sis. I think you should try to get down to see Randy today. He looks bad and is kind of loopy. The nurse says he could pass any time," Christy claimed.

"I'll try, but I can't get Nick to finish his school work and Mom is expecting me to get her to CVS for her pills. I swear I don't even know where Dad is, so I had better find out if he wandered off again. It's not fair that Kristen and Kaitlyn have to babysit their Grandpa. I *swear* I'm going to get down there first thing tomorrow, okay?"

"Okay,"

After talking to her mother and Lydia, Christy made Randy some soup, and he had a few bites, but then gave her the "time-out" signal when she tried to give him more, and said, "That's okay, I'm not really hungry now, maybe later." She didn't know it at the time, but that was the last meal Randy would have.

Randy was lucid and still had his sense of humor. He chatted a bit although Christy did have to give him some morphine. After a few such episodes, she suggested that he do a guided meditation with her. He was open to that as he had told her that his lungs felt like they were filling up with sand. He would try anything for relief. She had him recline, close his eyes and get comfortable, and asked him to imagine himself walking through a lovely landscape of his choice, perhaps strolling through a field of flowers, arriving at the edge of a beautiful lake. She asked him to see a large tree by the lake, that had a hammock just waiting for him to climb into. Then she suggested that he allow the breeze to simply rock the hammock, so he didn't have to do anything at all. It occurred to Christy to offer him the suggestion that he simply open his mouth and allow the breeze to breathe for him, any time his own breathing seemed labored. He calmed down throughout the meditation and seemed peaceful and content when she brought him back to linear time.

Rick had some soft music playing on the CD player and was trying to stay busy by puttering around the kitchen doing dishes, making tea and seeing if Christy needed anything.

The pastor from Rick's church came around 8 p.m., and he and Randy spent a few moments together in prayer and communion. When the pastor left, Randy had fallen asleep. Around 10 p.m. Randy started murmuring, questioning where he was. "Where am I? Am I home yet?"

"Yes, Randy. You are home in your bed. I'm here and Rick is in the kitchen," Christy assured him.

"Am I home? Did I make it home? Where am I?" he repeated.

"Yes, this is Christy, your sister. You are here at your home,"

Randy, as weak as he was, began to sit up in bed and clearly state: "Christy, I'm dying."

Trying to make light of the situation, she said: "You mean right now?"

"What am I afraid of?"

"I don't know. What do you think you are afraid of?"

He thought about his answer for quite some time. "I think that I am afraid that I didn't get to touch everyone."

Christy had no idea what this meant exactly. She felt powerless but she placed her hand underneath his and said, "I'll tell you what. How about you touch me now. Hold my hand. And I will make a promise to touch anyone you missed." She and Randy touched their foreheads together and spent awhile in silence. Then Randy said, "Well if I'm dying today, I want to be clean. Can you help me bathe and wash my hair?" Christy helped him into the bathroom, sat him on the shower stool, washed his hair, and scrubbed his back. Rick went in to help Randy with his more private areas. With a clean robe, they helped him lie back down.

Christy sat by his side for the three or four hours that Randy remained in his earthly body. He drifted off to sleep and although he never awoke, she was sure he could still hear her. Every time his breathing became labored and agitated, she whispered in his ear, "Randy, remember, you're in the hammock. Let the breeze breathe for you," and he would calm down immediately. She had on a continuous play of classical music, Randy's favorite, as she held his hand and gently chatted with him. She hoped a part of him was aware of how much she loved him. She had spoken with her mother earlier that day, alerting her to the fact that this was probably Randy's last day on earth. Marilyn had been stoic on the phone, but Christy could only imagine the grief and helplessness she must have been feeling.

It was time to call Marilyn and Lydia.

CHAPTER THIRTEEN

Regrets

When the phone rang in the middle of the night, Lydia reached across Vince's broad chest and knew instantly what the message on the other end of the line was. She hung up with her sister and whispered to Vince what he must have already known. She began to sob and he held her tight.

Something compelled him to begin caressing her, but not just out of comfort. He was kissing her like he did when they were young lovers. Her body began responding with the innocence of a young girl. There was something in Lydia that just needed to feel alive right then and there. She wasn't ready to mourn another death. For this brief moment, in the middle of the night, all she wanted was to feel loved and alive. Their lovemaking felt like a gift that she was badly in need of receiving.

The reality of the next morning hit hard. She was so angry with herself for not making the time to see Randy when Christy had asked her to.

I should have listened to Christy. I swore I was going to get there first thing today and I missed it. I missed saying goodbye.

I know Christy was there but I have been the one that has been here all those years that she was in Florida and California. I should have been there too!

She had to tell her children about their uncle and help with the care of Marilyn and Noel. Vince had work. There were bosses to call for days off. There was another funeral to prepare for.

Marilyn was quite concerned that Noel would be completely inappropriate at the funeral home so she and Lydia did not even tell Noel that Randy had passed away. Noel was so deep into the throes of his own disease that he really did not know who Randy was and would not have understood the concept of death. He had begun to wander around the neighborhood when not being watched and did not always make it to the bathroom on time. Noel often told his own grandchildren: "You don't belong here," no matter how many times it was explained that they lived there too. Trying to get him to follow even the most basic directions became burdensome.

For the viewing at the funeral home, Marilyn had asked the next -door neighbors if they would "babysit" him. The Thorpe children had never seen an open casket, yet Lydia thought that for ages 10, 7 and 5 they were real troopers. Christy wanted a picture of the open casket for her family that did not make it up from Florida and California. Lydia had never heard of such a strange request. Did people really take pictures of the dead in their casket? Rick looked amazing. He had on a navy blue suit and a tie with a nondescript print. But, he also looked haggard, as anyone would have who had just lost the love of their life.

The following days were very familiar to Lydia and Marilyn. There were relatives visiting and flowers being delivered. There were phone calls and sympathy cards in the mail for weeks after the real funeral. Because Randy and Rick had been together for so long, Randy's ashes were buried in a plot in Ohio where Rick would eventually be as well. No more long trips to the hills of Pennsylvania, as Marilyn had sold the extra Pennsylvania funeral plots years ago.

Noel seemed oblivious to the reasons all of these strangers were visiting and why there were cards and flowers everywhere. The children went back to doing their schoolwork, playing in the yard and being normal kids. Marilyn and Lydia tried to appear normal too, but they weren't. Marilyn had long given up her stoicism and cried at every little thing. The stress of the last few months had given her Parkinson's new fuel. She now needed her walker all the time, as well as help dressing and undressing, showering, and often needed help in the kitchen.

While Marilyn was dealing with her grief by crying and feeling helpless, Lydia was pushing her grief aside by being snarky and moody. She snapped at her husband, her kids and worst of all, she barked at the woman who needed the most to be treated with kid gloves, her own mother. Every day Lydia rushed through the needs of Marilyn so that she could get the kids started with their schoolwork and schedule her part-time hours at the rink. She lost sight of the emotional needs of everyone, including herself. Perhaps being a former distance runner, she assumed she could just power through everything like those last eight miles of a marathon. Being all things to all people was what her dad always tried to do before he began walking the complicated maze of Alzheimer's Disease. She wanted to be blissfully happy each day like her father was when she was growing up, but honestly, she could not even remember the last time he was sane enough to give her any great advice or the last time that he did not loop the same story, again and again, like when her CD player would get stuck on repeat track.

Her sanity came when Marilyn was introduced to a woman named Barb, whom she met through Vince's family. Barb was a middle-aged woman who had beaten breast cancer and was only working part-time. She had lots of time to enjoy the company of Marilyn and Noel, so she would frequently visit to play Scrabble and Rummikub with Marilyn. It was a nice reprieve for Liddy when Marilyn, Noel and Barb would go out to lunch.

Vince could see that his dear wife was becoming unraveled and often suggested that she go for a run or a bike ride. Liddy just assumed he wanted her to work off some of her stress fat and took offense to his suggestions. Besides, if she took time for herself, wouldn't the world stop turning?

Dear Randy,

I have no idea where to begin. I guess I want to apologize first. When we were kids I couldn't stand you. I think it had to do with loving Teddy so much. In my little pea-sized brain, I could not fathom having enough love for two brothers at once. But I also think it was because you were so smart and artistically talented. The jealousy ate me alive.

But then as I matured I saw that you were not showing off, but that you were just exercising all of the talents God gave you. Your love for our family was intense. It was robust, indestructible, passionate and deep.

I remember when you were 13 and I was seven. You had drawn a three-foot high Queen Elizabeth in her frock for art class. Each and every bead and lace ruffle was drawn onto it with all of its intricacies. It was like something right out of the Cleveland Museum of Art. The quality. The detail. The time and care that went into this piece took more patience than I will ever have. Now I realize that you had this patience with me.

When we were kids you let me call you names and judge your lifestyle. You let me tease you about your legs and the problems with anything that required endurance. You took grief from Teddy if you teased me back, knowing he would side with the little baby of the family. You took it all and maybe never even knew if I would grow to love you like I did Teddy.

REGRETS

Well, in case you didn't know it, I did! Through your thoughtful patience and understanding, I learned to step out of judgment. I learned that I can love more than one person at a time. I learned that although I wished for some of your talents, I had (or have) my own.

Thank you, Randy, for blessing this earth with your rich and full life. I'll see you again, I am sure of it.

Your kid sis,
Lydia

CHAPTER FOURTEEN

Noel

Noel was getting significantly worse. The plan to keep him at home until his natural death was not working out. It had been several days since Noel had bathed or changed clothes. It was often too difficult to argue with him or make him understand that he used to shower and change clothing every day.

"Daddy, it's me. Lydia. I'm your daughter. I just want to help you get a shower and clean clothes," she pleaded one afternoon.

"I think I'm okay. I don't know you."

"I am your daughter!"

By this point, Marilyn had stepped in to reassure him that it was okay and that she would come into the bathroom too. He continued to fight Lydia, and walked out of the room to get away from these two strange women. Lydia had had enough and began ripping his shirt off and trying to pull him into the bathroom forcefully. A fistfight ensued. Lydia had no idea of the built-up anger and frustration she had been harboring these last several months. She put her arm up when he went to hit her and she ended up hitting him on the side of his eye where there is no body fat. He began to bleed. The remorse was instant and profound. She began crying and begging Marilyn to let her take him to the hospital in case he needed a stitch above his eye. She adamantly refused, and between the two women, they got Noel to calm down enough to put a butterfly on it and just give him a sponge bath.

"Mom! I feel horrible. What if the cut was deeper than we thought? We have insurance. Why didn't you want us to see a doctor?" she asked.

"What if they thought you were abusing him and not defending yourself?"

"Oh, I didn't think of that."

"You hear about elder abuse all the time on the news and it never ends up well. Let's just get him ready for bed," Marilyn said.

They ended up at the hospital a few weeks later. Marilyn was in charge of the myriad of pharmaceuticals that they were on. Noel had his Alzheimer's drugs, but had also been taking Coumadin for years so that he could still run his marathons with his atrial flutter. One sunny afternoon Marilyn carefully unlocked the box where she kept their prescriptions. She was counting and cutting the pills according to directions, then dispensing them into the plastic pill containers marked by day as well as by morning, afternoon and evening. The phone rang and she hobbled over to get it. Moments later she came back and the month's worth of Coumadin was gone. Perhaps Noel thought they were little Smarties candies or M and M's. Either way, the family assumed he ate them and rushed him to the hospital about five miles from their home. He was given vitamin K and fresh frozen plasma, but for several weeks afterward, the family was warned to never let Noel near a knife and to not bother shaving him.

Bedtime was the worst part of the day for both Lydia and Noel. Noel did what is commonly called "sundowning." He would be more agitated, more confused and did not even know Marilyn by name, although he still recognized her to be someone he loved. This generally occurred when Lydia was trying to make sure the kids had put their school things away, make dinner for the family, pray that Vince did not come home crabby, and deal with Noel all at the same time. He had no idea who his grandchildren were and would often look right at little Nick and say: "Go away." Kristen would often come in from playing to announce that Grandpa was walking down the street again. Lydia would have to stop what she was doing and calmly convince him to follow her back home. It was not too difficult to do most of the time, but the straw that broke the proverbial camel's back was on Christmas Eve.

The Thorpe tradition was to go to Christmas Eve Service and then come home to watch the 1970, Albert Finney version of *Scrooge*. Marilyn was too tired to go and said that she would just stay home with Noel. The three kids were wonderful at the service and Lydia had her customary cry when the traditional Christmas hymns were played. When they returned home, Marilyn was frantic. "Where is your father?" Marilyn asked.

"How would I know? We literally just walked in the door," Liddy snapped.

"Well, I have not seen him for at least 20 minutes. I have called for him but I don't even know if he knows his own name anymore!"

"I know where he may have gone," offered Vince. "He seems to always walk the same way. I'll go get him."

Vince returned about 10 minutes later with Noel half frozen. "I found him walking up Wilson Mills in the dark," he said. On one of the coldest nights in Ohio, on a street with no streetlights and no sidewalks, Noel was walking in a black shirt, black pants and black socks stretched over his black shoes. No coat, no gloves or hat and no idea where he was going or why he was walking late at night.

There were other things that made the decision to put Noel in a nursing home more and more appealing. He had defecated on the couch once. He had answered the door to receive a Meals on Wheels meal on one of the days that Lydia worked and had proceeded to lose the meal before he walked into the room where

Marilyn was. She asked him who was at the door and he had no idea. For months the joke in the family was to see if something somewhere in the house would begin to stink, they assumed they would find the meal under the couch. They never did.

Marilyn and Lydia were exhausted. Vince was easily agitated and the three Thorpe children were the most active, overscheduled, homeschooled kids around. Christy had no intention of ever moving back to the Cleveland area and everyone was missing Randy. Randy was the buffer. He was the glue that kept everyone from biting each other's heads off. His absence was acute and Lydia's stress overwhelming.

The decision was made. Noel was moved to the Veterans' Nursing Home that was a one and a half hour drive from their home. There were dozens and dozens of closer nursing homes, but the Veterans Home was the most affordable since Noel was a Veteran of World War Two. On the days that Marilyn insisted on visiting Noel, all three kids and Lydia would load up the minivan with their school workbooks, snacks and coloring books. While Marilyn visited, the kids would do their schoolwork with Lydia in the large cafeteria. Lydia dreaded those days that Marilyn wanted to see her husband. She had emotionally detached from Noel when he could no longer make a complete sentence. It was just too hard to see that the man she had run all of those marathons with, shared all of those conversations about boys, God, and life in general, had turned into a shell of his former self.

Lydia was getting excited about her 40th birthday. She loved the fact that it was a big one. About four days prior to her big day and less than five months after Randy's death, Lydia got a call at work from her mother. Noel had a brain aneurysm and had passed away quickly. She was stunned. He had barely moved into the V.A. Home. She was still grieving Randy, who had just died in the summer.

When she returned home from work, Lydia did her best to keep spirits up for her young kids and her mother. She knew all too well that her organized mother had already planned out the memorial service, had pre-paid for the cremation and knew all of the people she needed to call to tell of his passing. All Lydia had to do was to show up. She was numb. She was stupefied.

She and Marilyn made calls for the rest of the day while the arrangements were made to bring the body back to the Cleveland area from the Veterans' Home. The following morning, Lydia decided to go for a run. She still worked out on occasion but had not done much more than two or three various workouts in the last month because of lack of time. With her running shoes tied she snuck out before her children awoke. It ended up being the strangest four miles that she had ever had. After the run, the dust came off of her diary. She had not written more than an occasional entry since her life had become so busy.

Turning 40 and having Daddy die in the same week was insane. I went for a run this morning and was expecting it to be fairly miserable because I have not done that distance in months and I have put on weight since Randy's death. I got only halfway down the street when I just felt so tall and slim. I felt a presence on my left. Living in the country, I kept thinking it was a dog or a deer or even a coyote following me. I kept looking over my shoulder expecting a dog or even another runner. I can't really describe the feeling very well. So I finally figured out that I think Daddy was running with me. I knew it was him because for the last year or so it has been so hard to remember anything good about Dad. All I kept going over in my head was his illness and his weirdness. I had blocked out all of the good times in order to just function. But there I was this morning, running and suddenly like a waterfall, a gush of great memories came pouring down on me. There were the races where we won the father/daughter division. There were the car rides to races where the only music we could agree on was Bach, the Beach Boys, Chicago or Joni Mitchell. Memories of him waking me up with his crazy routine of *"Everybody out of the pool, rise and shine, time for a new day!"* and memories of those intense conversations about God's love filled the rest of that run. I remembered telling him about all of my breakups and he would just say, *"And this too shall pass"* which he truncated from 2 Corinthians Chapter Four where it talks about troubles being momentary and that eternal glory will outweigh them all. I think it was something about keeping our eyes on things that are unseen and not seen. He had used that on Mom when Grandpa Abe had died. Well anyway, I could see his smiling face, hear his cheerful voice and know I was loved beyond measure. It was the eeriest, yet comforting run I have ever had. I couldn't wait to come home and tell Mom all about it.

Vince stepped up to where Randy used to be. He was amazing and strong for Lydia and his children. He took the initiative to help more than usual so that Marilyn and Lydia could make the arrangements for the cremation and memorial service. He cleaned the house for the arrival of Christy and her family, which now included her first grandchild.

The Memorial was the Saturday after Thanksgiving and the turnout was wonderful. More than 20 years had gone by since Lydia eeked out that awkward eulogy at her friend Charlie's funeral at the Mormon Church. Now she was much stronger in her faith and in her ability to speak in front of a crowd. Death was becoming more a part of life for her, and she was more than happy to be the first of the three people to speak about Noel.

She told the story of the four-mile run the day after his death and at the end, she invited everyone to accept Jesus into their hearts as her father had invited her to many years ago. The next to speak was Marilyn's friend, Barb. She had only known Noel after his Alzheimer's had set in, so she talked about how even in his illness he had taught her many things.

Barb read: "I learned to see things in a more gentle light that for him brought 'new' people into his life every day. I would cry just watching how he would sit at their kitchen table and look at Marilyn with such love in his eyes. He may not have known her name, but he knew she was his special friend and the love was still there. Noel taught me to listen carefully and tried to talk about anything and everything. I didn't always understand what point he was trying to get across, but I loved to hear him chatter, just the same. Sometimes, I would even egg him on just to hear him chatter. If there was music on the TV he would jump up and conduct the orchestra, or tap dance on the hardwood floor. I will always remember that man who would tap dance for me and talk to me as a dear friend. Thank you for being part of my life."

Christy rounded up the talks with lots of great stories about his feminism, his ability to teach morals by living them, and how he always took adverse situations and turned them into something positive. Just as Lydia had her father all to herself on those long runs, Christy had Noel all to herself on those car rides to and from private school after the two brothers were dropped off. She laughed remembering his penchant for bursting out into song and dancing at the most random times, and how he set the gold standard for an amazing and loving marriage to Marilyn.

The Thorpe kids were well behaved, but Kristen cried more than anyone during the service. It reminded Lydia of how hard Sue had cried at Teddy's funeral years ago. Kristen was not particularly close to her crazy grandfather, but perhaps the reality of two deaths in five months made such a bright child think deeper thoughts than she should have had to at that age.

Death does that, doesn't it? It makes us think deep thoughts. It makes us wonder about all of the "what if's" and makes us continually question the meaning of our lives. Conceivably that is what it is meant to do.

Letters to the Dead Men

The Sixth and Final Letter

Dear Daddy,

There is just so much to say to you. Do you have any idea how completely wonderful you were to all of us? It seems crazy to me that you had such a zero of a father figure and that you chose to perhaps overcompensate by being the most loving parent ever.

The four of us challenged you to be sure. You loved all of us through things like drugs, alternative lifestyles, sex outside of marriage, poor decisions in school and so much more. You did it with grace and never gave into your own beliefs. I think in church we were told that it is called agape love, and is the highest form of love there is.

I am 100 percent sure that only a strong faith in God could have taught you how to show that much love, through the disappointment you must have felt as we navigated through those ugly teenage and young adult years.

Your generosity also blows my mind as I think about how poorly the family print shop did in terms of financial success, yet none of our boyfriends, girlfriends or husbands ever lacked a job. If you saw one of our friends in need, a printing press position always magically seemed to open up. I even remember a time where you had lent me your three best cameras so that my friend and I could go and shoot some fun pictures with them. We had stopped by the pool at home to relax and I had left the cameras outside by accident as we drove back into the Heights. It rained. You spent hours and hours taking those cameras apart, wiping them down and restoring their ability to shoot pictures. I don't even remember a punishment. How you held your anger I will never know.

I also must remind you of a day at the print shop when I was a know-it-all teenager. Mom was in the front office and you were down in the basement developing film. You both used to have that completely dorky radio station on that played sappy stuff like Mel Torme, Frank Sinatra and Dean Martin. So you buzzed her on the intercom and told her to turn up her front office radio because they were playing "our song." Then ten minutes later you buzzed her again with the same request. So by the third time you buzzed mom to say: "They are playing our song," I picked up the intercom and my irascible self said: "Dad! You've said that like three times already," and you replied, "Honey, with your mother, every love song is our song." Wow. Just wow!

And now for the apology. I loved you so much more than I can express. I told you secrets and things that I would have never told mom. You and I were so alike with our propensity to be so silly and random and to have so many moods. We shared a desire to live life to the fullest, and so when your mental capacity started to decline, I could not handle it. It was too difficult for me to lose my best friend. Dad, that's not an excuse. It's just an explanation for why I was such a horrible caregiver to you when you really needed me. I yelled at you and got so easily frustrated when your Alzheimer's would not allow you to follow simple directions. I did the most minimal care when it should have been time to really step up and show you what I was made of. I failed you. I cannot remember the last really meaningful conversation we had. I cannot remember the last kind or sacrificial thing I did for you and yet I can think of dozens of times that you sacrificed something for me. You were like a mini-Jesus, right here in the flesh.

All I can do now is to write this letter and let you know that I am so sorry. I am sorry I did not show agape love to you. I displayed only a self-absorbed, conditional love, and for that I am truly remorseful. All I can promise you now is that I will move onward and upward. I will do my best to pay it forward with my own husband and children. I will be unyielding in my attempt to exemplify your grace, unbridled joy, tolerance and eternal optimism as I live out however many days God has blessed me with.

Your Dear Sweet, Little, White Rose,
Lydia

CHAPTER FIFTEEN

Unexpected Revelations

"Mom," Nick said for the second time. "MOM!" he shouted, this time exasperated.

Lydia snapped to attention. "What?", she said as she seemed to have been dozing in the glowing light of the yellow flames of the fire.

"Where were you?" he asked.

"Yeah," Kristen chimed in. "It's like you were in another world. Nick called you three or four times. Are you tired?"

"No, I guess I was just reminiscing. I was reflecting on all of the people who have walked in and out of our lives, I guess."

Christy moved her seat closer to the heat of the dying fire and adjusted her chair. Looking at Lydia she commented, "You were just staring off into the fire for the longest time. Did you hear any of our discussion about Mom's service tomorrow? Are we going to do an open mic after the pastor talks, or just the eulogies you and I prepared?"

"Hmm, I don't know. I guess we will see what the turnout is and play it by ear" she said, somewhat distracted by her own thoughts.

Vince began collecting the empty beer cans and turned the CD player off. "The batteries are low and I guess we should call it a night," he said.

Kristen and Kaitlyn pushed their chairs over to their father and followed Nick and his flashlight around the pond and back to the house. "Goodnight Mom. Goodnight Dad. Goodnight Aunt Christy," they called.

Teasingly Christy called back "Goodnight Johnboy" but the humor was lost on a generation who had never seen *The Walton's*.

Vince, Lydia, and Christy stayed a few more minutes to make sure that the fire died down enough to not be a danger, and as the flames began to wane down to tiny embers, Lydia spoke.

"Kaitlyn really had a great idea about those letters. Maybe I should write them to the ladies too. You know I miss Grandma and I know I will miss Mom. Did you know that Randy's partner died?"

"Oh, is that why his letters kept coming back to us?," Christy said.

"Yes. It would have been great to see him at Mom's memorial. When I could never get an answer from the only phone number I still had, as a last-ditch effort, I used the computer to look up obituaries and there he was. My friend Roger died too. He was the one who used to hang around Aaron in high school. I think he has been gone for about twelve years. What a shame he did not reach middle age." Lydia concluded.

"And what a misfortune that Barb's breast cancer came back. How long has it been since she has passed?" Christy asked.

"I'm guessing about seven years, now."

"Well, let's hope Mom's death is the last one for a while. I love visiting Cleveland, but someday I just want to come up here for a wedding or anniversary instead of a funeral."

Unexpected Revelations

"Amen to that," Liddy said.

The embers were mere specks. Vince had all of the beer cans and empty chip bags in a backpack to take to the garage trash bin. He threw it over one shoulder as Christy lit up her cell phone to see her way through the grass, twigs, and branches around the pond.

Once inside, Lydia rummaged around in her Mother's old room, which she had now begun using as an office. She found an unused composition book and resurrected her diary writing.

How corny and cliché it sounds to say Dear Diary, but here it is.

Dear Diary,

Tonight I unpacked some thoughts that I had no idea where they had been stored. What has been revealed to me was that as I experienced each finality and irreversible ending of a life, it tore me into small pieces that I kept storing into little compartments of myself. I tried to ignore those fragments. Maybe I thought If I could keep all of those little pieces in separate chambers, perhaps they would remain small and insignificant. Heaven forbid that all of that loss be stored in one place, one pool, for perhaps I might drown in it. So like a coat with several pockets, each death was stored away where they remained hidden as I continued to live the only way I knew how to, by muscling through it. But eventually, we must grieve. We must learn that grief can not be stored away and must be dealt with head-on.

Where there was guilt, I must forgive.
Where there was pain, I must acknowledge it.
Where there was a big, gaping hole of emptiness, I must admit it instead of hiding it.
Ah, but where there was joy and love I must boldly show the living that delightful side of them through me.

As I see it, we always have at least two choices. Yes or No? Black or White? Chocolate or Vanilla? Hide the pain or concede to it? I think on this night I choose to be privileged to embrace grief for all its magnificence. Once we admit to life's transient nature, we can boldly move forward and become the best version of ourselves we can be. From this day forward I will consider it an honor to grieve with the understanding that it is an ongoing process but that it does not have to define me.

Credits

* "My Dog Is A Plumber," by Dan Greenburg. Copyright © 1972, Free To Be Foundation, Inc. From the collection, *Free To Be... You And Me,* used by permission. www.FreeToBeFoundation.com

Acknowledgments

No book is ever written simply from the mind of the writer. There are always people in the background supporting in so many ways. Friends, family, financial backers, editors, cover designers, formatting artists, marketing people, beta readers and people who simply put up with you when all you can talk about is the book, the book, the book...

It was my great privilege to have so many believe in me as I set out to honor the people I wrote about in this work. I want to sincerely thank the following people who helped tremendously, also knowing there were so many others who supported this project.

To my sister Christine Wines, I owe you my eternal love and gratitude. I see the best parts of Daddy in you. To my husband Vince, thank you for putting *Letters to the Dead Men* in my head that one afternoon that I ceased to truncate my story. To Connie Swenson, thank you for making me a better writer and being honest at all times. To Kris Fondran, you too, like Vince, planted a writing seed in me years ago. I scoffed at it then, but here I am writing. To Alan and Sandy Lane, your financial support has not only been a great help, but the salvation of my soul even greater. Thanks for leading me back to Christ in 1985. To Rob Petras, you always knew what to say as I dealt with life's challenges. You are one of those forever friends. To Karen Hostoffer, I am so delighted that our friendship went well beyond those crazy summer swim meets. To June Hudnall, I hope the story of Grandpa Abe touched you as he was truly a man who lived Peace With Justice. To Tricia Landon Kuivinen, I am honored that what started as a provider and client relationship is now so very much more. And, to Jennifer Vilimonovic, I hope you enjoy my writing as much as I enjoy your beautiful music, friendship and lovely spirit.

www.ingramcontent.com/pod-product-compliance
Lightning Source LLC
LaVergne TN
LVHW041639060526
838200LV00040B/1629